A Novices Guide

to Wealth

Design Your Financial Life with Tax Clarity, Asset Protection, and Purpose.

Dedication

To my incredible wife, whose unwavering love, strength, and belief in me gave me the courage to begin again, this book is as much yours as it is mine.

To my children, who are my daily inspiration and the reason I strive for a better future, may you always value health, purpose, and resilience above all.

To my sister, whose quiet support and steadfast presence reminded me I was never alone.

To my nephew, who brings light, joy, and renewed hope into my life.

To my mother, whose wisdom and prayers formed the foundation I stand on, your sacrifices will never be forgotten.

To my late father, whose values, strength, and quiet guidance continue to shape the man I strive to be, your legacy lives on in every word of this book and every step I take forward.

To my friends and colleagues, thank you for your encouragement, your patience, and your belief in this journey. Each of you played a part in helping me rebuild not just my wealth, but my life.

This book is dedicated to all of you, with gratitude, love, and deep respect.

Acknowledgements

This book would not have been possible without the guidance, wisdom, and generosity of many individuals to whom I am deeply grateful.

First and foremost, I would like to express my heartfelt thanks to the mentors, professionals, and educators who generously shared their knowledge and insights in the fields of wealth management, estate planning, taxation, and insurance. Your expertise helped shape my understanding and gave me the foundation upon which this book was built.

To the financial planners, tax advisors, estate attorneys, and insurance specialists who took the time to answer my many questions, clarify complex strategies, and share real-world experiences, thank you. Your practical insights bridged the gap between theory and application in ways no textbook could.

A special note of gratitude goes to:

- **Arron Bennett**, CEO & CFO, *Bennett Financials*- "Numbers Whisperer"

- **Dennis Drake**, Certified Tax and Business Advisor

- **Sunny Mitra**, Wealth Consultant, *Atlanta First Guarantee* -"Turn Your Tax Liabilities Into Assets"

- **Michael Notbohm**, *Legacy Wealth Code*

- **Michael D. Aguas**, *Reignstorm Group*

- **John Brooke**, President, *Cash Flow Mastered* - "Cash Flow Optimization for Entrepreneurs"

- **Jake Mellor**, CEO, *AlphaMark Capital*

- **Toby Mathis**, Asset Protection and Tax Advisor, *Anderson*

- **Troy Lucas**, Managing Associate, *Opes One*

- **Vijayjit Virk**, Managing Associate, *Opes One*

- **Kuldeep Madan** - M+

- **Alex Aderman** - M+

Your guidance and support went beyond technical knowledge, offering encouragement, challenge, and perspective at just the right moments.

To my peers and colleagues, thank you for the thought-provoking conversations, late-night brainstorming, and shared passion for helping others navigate financial complexity with clarity and confidence.

Lastly, I extend my appreciation to the countless friends and reviewers.

Thank you all for being part of this journey. This work is a reflection of your influence, and I am deeply grateful.

Disclaimer

The information provided in this book is based on my personal journey, experiences, and interpretations of various financial strategies that I learned along the way. I am not a certified professional accountant, licensed financial advisor, attorney, or tax professional.

Thus, the insights shared throughout this book are intended solely for informational purposes and also to serve as a means to help you start earning and saving more effectively.

In no way should these strategies be interpreted as professional financial advice.

While I have made every effort to present strategies and concepts that are legal, ethical, and grounded in research, it's still important to understand that financial laws and regulations are subject to change and vary across jurisdictions.

Therefore, before making any financial decisions involving taxes, investments, insurance, real estate planning, or legal structures, I strongly recommend consulting with qualified financial or accounting professionals who are familiar with your individual situation and local laws.

Your financial journey is unique. Please use this book as a starting point to ask better questions, seek trusted guidance, and make informed decisions that are in line with your goals and values.

Thank You!

Table of Contents

Introduction

When Time Stops, A Heartbeat Away from a Wake-Up Call

There comes a moment in life that is so still, so silent, so terrifying, it forces everything to pause. For me, that moment wasn't poetic or symbolic. It was literal. My heart rate dropped to zero. I flatlined. I was clinically dead... and then brought back to life. Not just once, but several times.

It wasn't a heart attack. It was bradycardia, a condition I had barely heard of until it took control of my life. I now live because of a small machine implanted in my chest, a pacemaker that keeps my heart beating. But in that hospital bed, as alarms buzzed and machines blinked, I wasn't thinking about the science behind my survival. I was thinking about my wife, Pallavi, and our children, Anushka and Ashank. I was thinking, what happens to them if I don't wake up?

Despite the fact that I was doing well financially, despite the comfortable life we had built, I had no will. No trust. No life insurance. No roadmap. If I had died that night, I would have left behind a mess. A mess made of unanswered questions, financial uncertainty, legal complications, and a painful void in the lives of the people who mattered most.

In that moment, I saw the brutal difference between income and protection. Between doing well and being prepared.

Success, I realized, isn't just about how much you make. It's about how much you preserve, how well you protect it, and how wisely you pass it on.

I'm not a financial advisor. I'm not a CPA. I don't have formal financial training. But I do have something else. I have an obsession. The kind of obsession that only someone who's faced death and come back can truly understand.

I read everything I could. I listened, I studied, I questioned. I started researching tax laws, wealth strategies, insurance solutions, asset protection, estate planning, and everything in between. What I found shocked me. There's an entire world of tools and techniques available, legal, ethical, and incredibly effective, but they're often reserved for the wealthy, hidden behind professional jargon and financial gatekeepers. The truth is, the tax code isn't broken. It's simply a game that most people don't know how to play. But once you understand the rules, everything changes.

This isn't just theory. Consider the estate of legendary musician Prince. When he died without a will in 2016, his estimated $156 million estate became entangled in court for over six years. Much of it was lost to legal fees and taxes, and heirs had to wait nearly a decade for resolution. That's the reality of dying without a plan.

This book is my way of handing you those rules, not from the perspective of an expert, but from someone who had to learn it all the hard way. My goal is simple: to help others avoid the mistakes I made and build a life that is not just financially successful, but protected, intentional, and free.

Throughout this journey, I've discovered that most high-income individuals fall into two broad paths. There are those who earn strong salaries through W2 employment and try to build passive income on the side. Then there are those who own businesses and must navigate the complexity of entrepreneurship, taxes, and long-term growth. Each of these paths comes with its own challenges, and each one demands a different strategy. This book gives you both.

But let me be clear. This isn't a book about getting rich quickly. It's not about clever loopholes or gaming the system. It's about freedom. The freedom to live without fear. The freedom to give with purpose. The freedom to pass on more than just material wealth. It's about building a legacy that can survive you.

I believe that between birth and death lies the most powerful force we control, choice. And when we choose with clarity, with purpose, and with knowledge, we step into something greater than financial comfort. We step into economic freedom.

If you're holding this book, it means you still have time. You don't have to wait for a health scare or a close call to wake up. You can start now. You don't need to be a millionaire to think like one. You don't need a financial degree to take control of your future.

You just need to make the choice. To prepare. To protect. To build.

You also don't need to wait until you're older or already earning six figures to begin. The earlier you start, even as a young professional in your 20s or 30s, the more powerful these strategies become over time. This book isn't just for high earners trying to lower their tax bill; it's also for the rising professionals who want to avoid financial traps before they begin. Whether you're already at the top of your career or just starting out, the principles of economic freedom apply.

Let's begin.

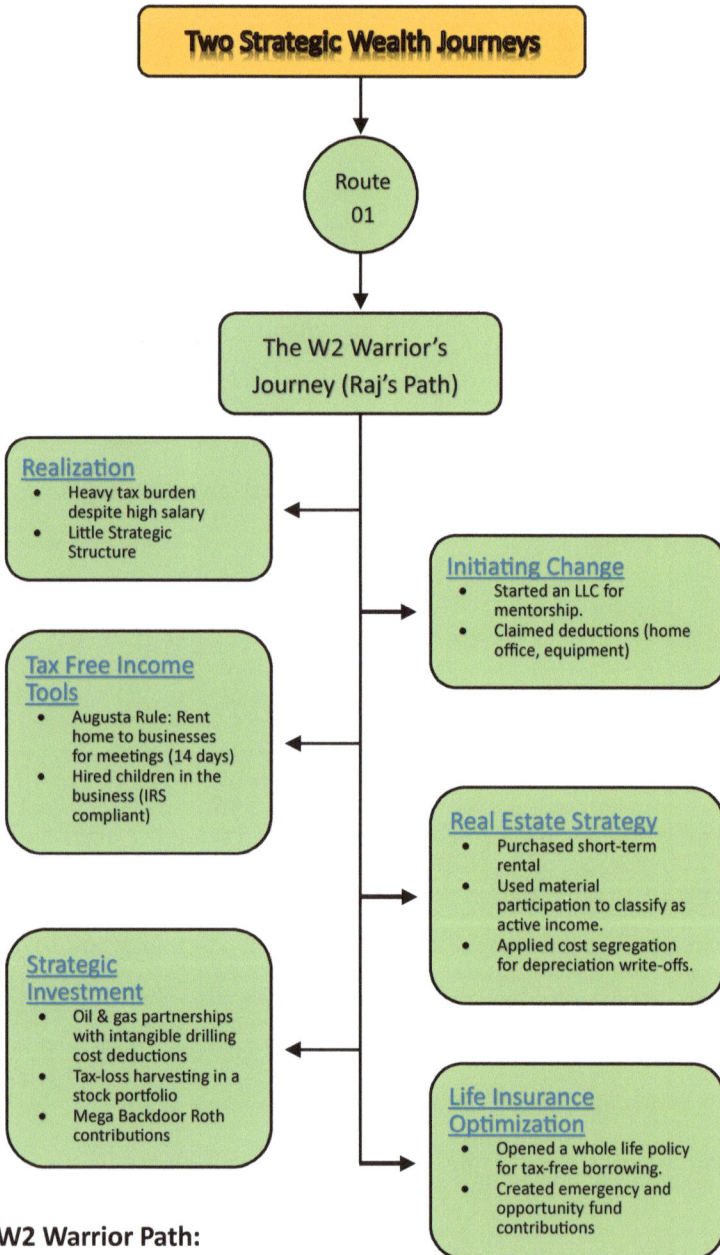

Two Strategic Wealth Journeys

Route 01

The W2 Warrior's Journey (Raj's Path)

Realization
- Heavy tax burden despite high salary
- Little Strategic Structure

Initiating Change
- Started an LLC for mentorship.
- Claimed deductions (home office, equipment)

Tax Free Income Tools
- Augusta Rule: Rent home to businesses for meetings (14 days)
- Hired children in the business (IRS compliant)

Real Estate Strategy
- Purchased short-term rental
- Used material participation to classify as active income.
- Applied cost segregation for depreciation write-offs.

Strategic Investment
- Oil & gas partnerships with intangible drilling cost deductions
- Tax-loss harvesting in a stock portfolio
- Mega Backdoor Roth contributions

Life Insurance Optimization
- Opened a whole life policy for tax-free borrowing.
- Created emergency and opportunity fund contributions

W2 Warrior Path:

W2 Earner → Strategic Side Hustle → Tax Optimization → Passive Income → Wealth Structure

Two Strategic Wealth Journeys

Route 02

The Business Builder's Blueprint (Priya's Path)

Realization
- Business success ≠ optimized tax structure
- High income = high tax liability

Entity Optimization
- Transformed from LLC to S-Corp → Saved payroll taxes
- Considered C-Corp for reinvestment strategies

Smart Deductions
- Used Section 179 + Bonus Depreciation on equipment
- Paid children through the business
- Applied the Augusta Rule for home rental

Medical and Insurance Leverage
- Set up MERP for tax-free medical expense reimbursements
- Used business-funded life insurance for cash growth + exit strategy

Asset and Retirement Planning
- Implemented vehicle logging and equipment financing
- Opened Solo 401(k) and Defined Benefit Plan (high contribution limits)

Real Estate and Charitable Strategy
- Used cost segregation on commercial buildings
- Opened Donor-Advised Fund with appreciated stock

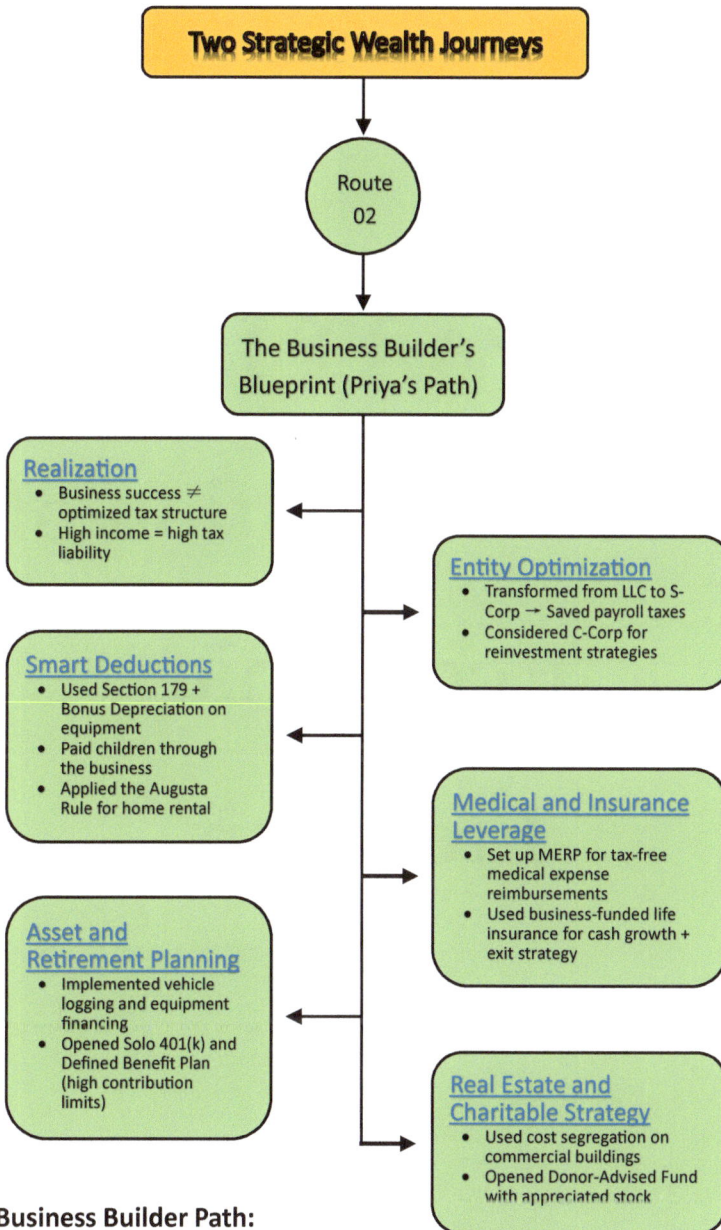

Business Builder Path:

Business Growth → Entity Structuring → Tax Strategy → Family Wealth Systems → Purpose-Driven Wealth Planning

PART I:

The Foundation of

Economic

Freedom

Chapter 1: The Illusion of Safety: Why High Income ≠ Wealth

If you earn a high income, you've probably been told, either by society or your own assumptions, that you've made it. Maybe you've landed a top job in tech, finance, medicine, law, or business. Your LinkedIn profile looks sharp, your paycheck is impressive, and your friends and family see you as successful. You've upgraded your car, your home, and your vacations. On the surface, everything signals "you've won."

But what if I told you that most high-income earners are one medical emergency, one economic downturn, or one unexpected life event away from financial vulnerability?

It sounds dramatic, but I've lived it. And I'm telling you now, high income is not the same as wealth.

I believed I was doing well. I had a strong job, consistent pay, savings, and a few investments. But when my heart literally stopped beating due to bradycardia, the illusion of safety cracked wide open. I was lying in a hospital bed with a machine keeping me alive, and for the first time, I saw the full picture.

I had no estate plan. No will. No life insurance. No financial structure to protect my wife, Pallavi, or our children, Anushka and Ashank, if I didn't come back. All the income in the world meant nothing if it couldn't secure their future.

That was my wake-up call. This chapter is your invitation to wake up, before life forces it on you.

In this chapter, we're going to break through that illusion. We'll examine the core myths that keep high-income earners from building real wealth and look at the structural disadvantages W2 professionals face. We'll explore how taxes quietly erode your gains while you're focused on working harder. Most importantly, you'll learn how to begin auditing your financial life; not just to count dollars, but to build clarity, control, and confidence.

Here's what we'll cover in this chapter:

- The critical difference between income and wealth
- Why W2 earners are structurally limited unless they take action
- How taxes are the silent killer of long-term wealth

- How to understand and audit your current financial position so you can take strategic control

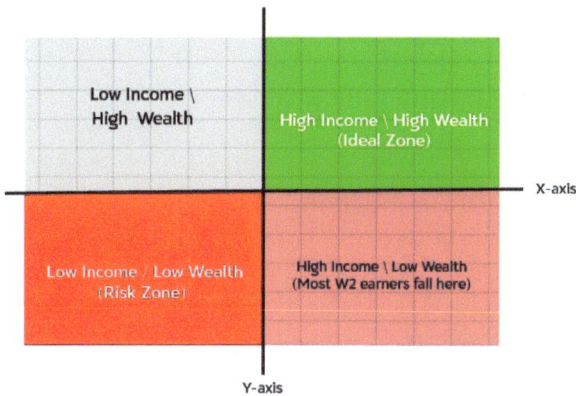

Income vs Wealth Matrix

Low Income \ High Wealth

High Income \ High Wealth (Ideal Zone)

X-axis

Low Income / Low Wealth (Risk Zone)

High Income \ Low Wealth (Most W2 earners fall here)

Y-axis

The Dangerous Lie We've Been Sold

Growing up, we're sold a simple story. Go to school, get good grades, find a high-paying job, and life will take care of itself. And for many of us, that story works, up to a point.

You get the degree. You get the job. The paycheck starts rolling in. You lease the car, buy the house, maybe even start investing a little on the side. Your income climbs, your confidence grows, and your lifestyle rises to match.

But deep down, you know something isn't right. You're working harder than ever, but your taxes feel heavier, your time feels shorter, and the security you expected to feel never fully arrives. That's because you're living in the illusion of safety, confusing high income with wealth.

Income is active. It requires your time, your presence, and your energy. Wealth is passive. It works for you, whether you're awake or asleep, healthy or not. Wealth doesn't just look good on a pay stub; it feels good in the form of ownership, options, and peace of mind.

Until you understand the difference, you'll always be working harder, not smarter.

And here's the good news: you don't have to wait until you're a high-income earner to start thinking like one. In fact, the earlier you start understanding these principles, before lifestyle creep, big tax bills, or bad investments, the stronger your financial foundation becomes. This chapter is for every earner who wants to work smarter, not just harder.

W2 vs Business: A Game of Unequal Rules

Let's talk about the two major camps in the world of high earners: W2 employees and business owners.

W2 professionals are the backbone of the economy. Doctors, engineers, executives, consultants, tech leads, lawyers, they're highly skilled and highly paid. But the moment they earn a dollar, the government takes a bite. Federal tax, state tax, Social Security, and Medicare are gone before that dollar ever hits their bank account. Then come the limitations. Limited deductions. Limited retirement tools. Limited ways to reduce their tax burden.

Business owners, on the other hand, play a very different game. They earn income, but they also control how it's received and how it's categorized. They pay expenses first, such as office space, equipment, payroll, vehicles, travel, and insurance, and then they're taxed on what's left. They can reinvest, defer, depreciate, and legally structure their financial world in ways that can reduce their tax burden significantly.

This isn't about fairness. It's about knowing the rules.

W2 earners are not doomed. But to win, they have to be intentional. They must learn to use the right strategies, build entities, diversify income streams, and take full advantage of what the tax code allows when approached with the right mindset.

Feature	W2 Earners	Business Owners
Taxed On	Gross income	Net profit (after expenses)
Flexibility on Deductions	Very limited	Extensive
Retirement Plan Options	Mostly employer-sponsored	Self-directed (Solo 401k, SEP IRA)
Payroll Taxes	Required	Optimizable (S-Corp)
Control Over Income Timing	None	High

Tax Rate Comparison Bar Graph

Tax Rate Comparison: Active vs Passive vs Capital Gains

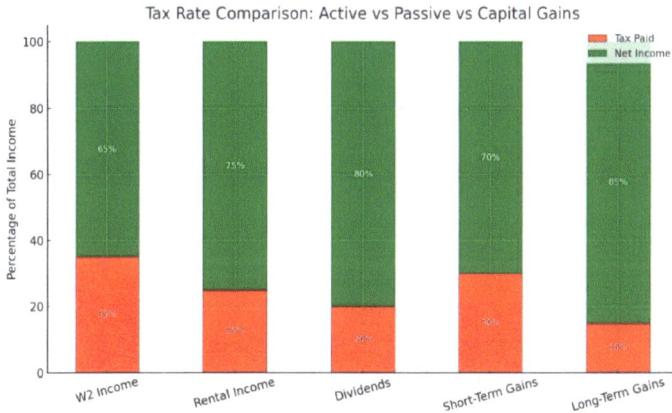

The Silent Killer: Taxes

Here's the part no one wants to talk about.

It's not lifestyle inflation that kills wealth. It's taxes.

Taxes are the silent, relentless drain on your income. And the more you earn, the more they take. You're not being punished for doing well; you're just uninformed about how the system rewards different behaviors.

The U.S. tax code isn't evil. It's strategic. It incentivizes what the government wants more of: business ownership, housing, job creation, clean energy, and charitable giving. It penalizes

W2 income because it doesn't contribute to those areas in the same way.

A recent report by the *Tax Foundation* highlights that the top 1% of income earners pay over 42% of all federal income taxes, Their average tax rate was **25.9%**, significantly higher than the **3.3%** paid by the bottom half of taxpayer, while having limited access to the kinds of deductions and tax shelters available to business owners.

That statistic becomes even more staggering when you realize how few of those earners are using the strategies shared in this book.

If you don't understand this, you'll keep trading time for money, only to give a third to half of it away each year, and wonder why real wealth never arrives.

Start with Clarity: Audit Your Financial Landscape

Most people avoid looking too closely at their finances because they're afraid of what they'll find. However, the first step to building lasting wealth is awareness.

You need to know how your financial life is actually structured, not what it looks like from the outside, but how it operates beneath the surface.

Start by asking yourself the hard questions:

- How much am I paying in taxes annually, and why?
- What percentage of my income is passive versus earned?
- Do I have a legal entity that can help me manage income differently?
- Am I using deductions, depreciation, and deferrals effectively?
- Do I have an estate plan, a trust, or even basic life insurance?
- If I stopped working tomorrow, how long would my financial plan survive?

Tools like Rocket Money can help you track spending, subscriptions, and recurring charges. But you'll need more than that. You'll need a tax strategist who thinks about the future, not just the past. You'll need an estate planner who sees your legacy, not just your net worth. You'll need to treat your life like a business and start building a financial team accordingly.

The good news is, you don't need to do it all at once. But you do need to start.

The Choice You Must Make

You can't control how much you're taxed. But you can control how you structure your life to minimize the impact. You can control your decisions, your strategy, and your mindset.

There is no safety in high income without a strategy. There is no wealth without protection. And there is no freedom without structure.

Most people never learn this until it's too late. But you're not most people.

You've seen what can happen when life changes in an instant. You've felt the pressure of responsibility, the weight of uncertainty. That's why you're here.

The illusion of safety ends here.

Let's start building something real.

Now that we've broken down the illusion of safety and looked at the cracks in a high-income, low-strategy approach, it's time to get specific.

In the next chapter, we'll demystify the tax system. You'll learn the difference between active and passive income, how capital gains differ from ordinary income, and how your Adjusted Gross Income (AGI) can be optimized to open doors to powerful tax-saving strategies.

Most importantly, you'll begin to see taxes not as a burden, but as a tool; one that can work for you when you understand how to use it.

Let's turn the page and begin learning the rules of the Tax game.

Chapter 2: Understanding the Tax Game

When I first started looking seriously at my finances after my heart incident, I thought taxes were just something to endure. I used to see the tax system as being like gravity, unavoidable and indifferent. You earn, the government takes, and you move on. That's the price of living in a developed society, right?

But that mindset almost cost me everything.

What I realized, slowly at first, is that taxes aren't just a civic duty. They are a game, one that most people lose not because they're dishonest or lazy, but because they never learn the rules. I wasn't trying to cheat the system. I just didn't know how the system actually worked. And unfortunately, I was like most high-income earners: working harder, paying more, and feeling stuck.

Once I began digging into tax strategy, not from YouTube gurus but from IRS publications, legal tax codes, and conversations with advisors who work with the ultra-wealthy, I saw the truth. The system is full of opportunities for those who understand it. And if you want to build true wealth, understanding the tax game is not optional. It is essential.

In this chapter, we'll cover some of the core concepts that underpin everything else in this book. You don't need to be a CPA to follow along. You just need to be willing to think differently, more strategically, more like the wealthy.

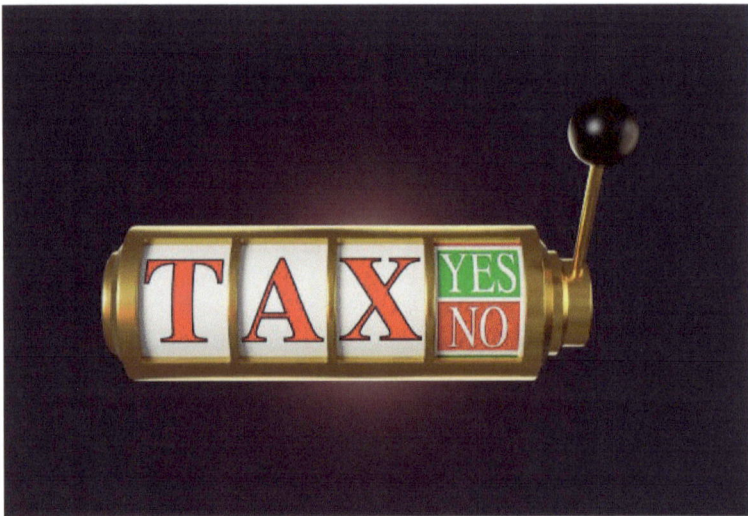

The Two Types of Income, Active and Passive

At the heart of the tax game is the question: What kind of income are you earning?

There are two basic types: active income and passive income.

Active income includes your salary, wages, tips, commissions, and any money you earn by directly trading your time and effort. This is the income most people are familiar with, and it's also taxed the most aggressively. If you're earning a high six- or seven-figure W2 salary, you're likely giving up 35% or more to taxes. And if you live in a high-tax state? Add another 8%–13%.

Passive income, on the other hand, is generated from investments like rental properties, dividends, royalties, or partnerships where you're not materially involved. It's income that doesn't demand your daily presence. And here's the kicker, it's usually taxed at lower rates and often comes with powerful deductions.

Let that sink in. The tax code favors those who earn money without working for it every day. It rewards those who build systems, not those who clock in.

This is why one of the first strategies of the wealthy is to shift income from active to passive. You don't need to quit your job to do this. You just need to start allocating time and money toward income streams that grow without you.

Feature	Active Income (W2 / Salary)	Passive Income (Rental / Investments)
Tax Rate	Highest marginal rate (up to 37% + state)	Often lower (15%–20% capital gains, or offset with deductions)
Subject to Payroll Taxes?	Yes (Social Security & Medicare)	No
Time Required	Ongoing personal effort	Minimal once systems are set
Eligible for Deductions?	Limited (W2)	Broader (depreciation, interest, maintenance, etc.)
Common Examples	Salary, bonuses, consulting fees	Rental income, royalties, dividends, and limited partnerships

Ordinary Income vs. Capital Gains

Now, let's add another layer: ordinary income versus capital gains.

Ordinary income is what you earn from your job, side hustle, or business profit. It's taxed at your regular income tax bracket, up to 37% federally, plus state taxes.

Capital gains are profits made from selling assets, stocks, real estate, and businesses. If you sell an asset you've held for less than a year, it's a short-term capital gain and taxed as ordinary income. But if you hold that asset for more than a year, it qualifies as a long-term capital gain, taxed at a much lower rate: 0%, 15%, or 20%, depending on your total income.

Here's an example: If you sell $500,000 worth of stock that you held for over a year, you could pay just 15% in federal taxes, $75,000. But if you earned that $500,000 as salary, you might pay over $180,000 in combined federal and state taxes.

Same dollar amount. Wildly different outcomes.

This is why wealthy people don't just make money. They hold it strategically. They sell strategically. And they understand that the classification of income can be just as important as the amount.

The Power of AGI, Deductions, and Credits

Another important term you must understand is Adjusted Gross Income (AGI). This number determines your tax bracket and your eligibility for certain deductions and credits.

AGI is calculated by taking your gross income (everything you earned) and subtracting certain deductions like:

- Traditional IRA or 401(k) contributions
- Health Savings Account (HSA) contributions
- Student loan interest
- Self-employed health insurance

Once you reduce your AGI, your tax liability often goes down. That's why high earners focus not just on income, but on optimizing AGI. This opens the door to:

- Lower effective tax rates
- Bigger deductions (such as charitable giving or business expenses)
- Eligibility for certain credits that might otherwise phase out

Next, understand the difference between deductions and credits. A deduction reduces your taxable income. A credit reduces your actual tax bill, dollar for dollar.

So, a $10,000 deduction might save you $3,000 in taxes. But a $10,000 credit saves you $10,000. Big difference.

Some of the most powerful credits available include:

- Energy-efficient home upgrades
- Electric vehicle credits
- Adoption credits
- Clean energy investments
- Certain business hiring incentives

The tax game isn't about cheating. It's about knowing what the system rewards, and aligning your actions with those incentives.

The Rules Are Written, Just Not Widely Read

One of the most eye-opening things I learned is that the tax code is full of rewards, not just punishments.

Want to reduce your taxes?

Start a business, invest in housing, employ others, support charities, and fund innovation.

These are the behaviors the government wants to encourage, so the tax code supports them. But most people don't do these things. They just keep earning, spending, and filing, without ever asking, "Is there a smarter way?"

You don't need to become an accountant. You need to become a student of your own financial system. Once you understand that every financial decision has a tax consequence, you begin to think differently about how you earn, spend, invest, and give.

Where It All Begins

Understanding the tax game is foundational to building wealth. Not because taxes are bad, but because they are powerful, and because most people treat them passively.

You're not like most people. You're reading this book because you've decided to act with intention. You've decided to take responsibility for what happens next. And that means learning how to design your income, not just earn it.

You've now seen the key differences between types of income, the importance of AGI, and how the tax system rewards strategic behavior.

In the next chapter, we'll apply these principles to a real-world story.

You'll meet Raj, a high-earning W2 professional with no deductions, no strategy, and a mounting tax burden. Through his journey, you'll discover exactly how W2 earners can level the playing field, take control of their tax outcome, and begin the shift toward lasting wealth.

PART II:

Two Roads, One Destination – Choose Your Route to Wealth

Chapter 3: Route 1 – The W2 Warrior's Journey

Raj had done everything the world told him to do. He was educated, hardworking, and disciplined. As a senior software engineer earning over a million dollars annually in salary, stock options, and bonuses, he was the kind of success story most immigrant families dream about. He had the house in a prime ZIP code, the sleek electric car, and a retirement portfolio that looked impressive on paper.

And yet, every April, he dreaded one thing: his tax bill.

In 2024, Raj paid more than $400,000 in federal and state taxes. Despite earning seven figures, he felt like he was spinning on a wheel, working harder, paying more, and keeping less. His CPA shrugged and said, "You're a high-income W2 earner. This is just how it is."

But Raj couldn't shake the feeling that something was off. If the wealthy paid far less in taxes as a percentage of their income, how were they doing it? What did they know that he didn't?

That question marked the beginning of Raj's transformation. He didn't need to become a tax expert. He just needed to understand that high income without structure is a trap. Like many high-earning professionals, Raj had confused income with wealth. But real wealth isn't just about how much you make, it's about how much you keep, protect, and grow.

The W2 Dilemma

W2 employees like Raj are taxed at the highest rates, often with the fewest deductions. Every paycheck he received had already been sliced by federal income tax, state income tax, Social Security, and Medicare. He had little flexibility to defer income, claim deductions, or offset his earnings with creative strategies.

Unlike business owners, who get to deduct expenses before calculating taxable income, W2 earners are taxed first, then allowed to live on what remains.

Raj knew he had to change how he approached his finances. He didn't need to quit his job. He just needed to think like a business owner and start structuring his financial life with intention.

Building the W2 Warrior Playbook

Raj's first step was building a side business based on something he was already doing, mentoring young software developers. He registered a single-member LLC and began earning 1099 income. This side hustle, though small in revenue, opened the door to big deductions.

He set up a home office, documented its square footage, and began deducting a portion of his rent, internet, and utilities. He purchased a laptop, ergonomic chair, and second monitor for his business, all legitimate write-offs.

With even just $20,000 in annual 1099 income, Raj could now claim business deductions that lowered his overall Adjusted Gross Income (AGI). This brought him into a lower marginal tax bracket and opened the door to further strategies.

Next, Raj learned about the Augusta Rule, which allows homeowners to rent their personal residence to a business for up to 14 days per year without claiming the income. He held quarterly planning retreats for his side hustle at his home, documented the fair market rental rate, and paid himself nearly $15,000 in tax-free income annually.

Then came his children. Raj had two kids, ages 12 and 14. He hired them to help with basic admin work, filing receipts, assembling slide decks, and editing videos for his business.

Paying them a reasonable wage (within IRS guidelines) shifted income from his high bracket to their 0% tax bracket, and he deposited part of their earnings into custodial Roth IRAs. His kids learned real-life financial skills, and Raj reduced his taxable income while building a generational wealth mindset.

Unlocking Real Estate as a W2 Earner

Raj wanted to expand beyond consulting, so he purchased a short-term rental property near a national park. With smart management and a bit of Airbnb strategy, he achieved over 100 nights of bookings in the first year.

Here's where things got interesting.

Most W2 earners can't use real estate losses to offset their income. However, short-term rentals have a special carve-out: if rented for less than an average of seven days and if you materially participate, the income can be considered non-passive.

Raj hired a CPA who understood this. Through cost segregation, he accelerated depreciation on the property, splitting the building into components like flooring, appliances, and HVAC systems. This allowed him to claim over $60,000 in paper losses in the first year. And because the income was treated as active, he used those losses to offset his W2 earnings.

Even better, his wife, Pallavi, who had stepped away from full-time work, qualified as a Real Estate Professional by actively managing the property. This status unlocked more deductions, as the IRS allowed her participation to "flow through" to their joint return.

Investing for Tax Optimization

Raj didn't stop at real estate. He diversified into oil and gas partnerships, which come with something called intangible drilling costs. These are often 100% deductible in year one, even against W2 income. He invested $50,000 and legally deducted the full amount, shrinking his tax bill and adding a passive income stream.

He also worked with a financial advisor to implement tax loss harvesting, selling underperforming investments to offset capital gains elsewhere in his portfolio.

Finally, Raj discovered that his company's retirement plan allowed a Mega Backdoor Roth. This lets him contribute up to $66,000 annually to a Roth account, growing tax-free forever. He also used ERISA-protected accounts for his side hustle, building a tax-deferred savings shielded from lawsuits and creditors.

Becoming His Own Bank

Raj's final move was perhaps the most powerful. He opened a high cash value whole life insurance policy, structured for maximum liquidity, not a death benefit. Within a few years, he had a six-figure cash value he could borrow against tax-free to invest in more real estate or fund future ventures.

It became his emergency fund, his opportunity fund, and his legacy plan, all in one.

Raj's Transformation Timeline

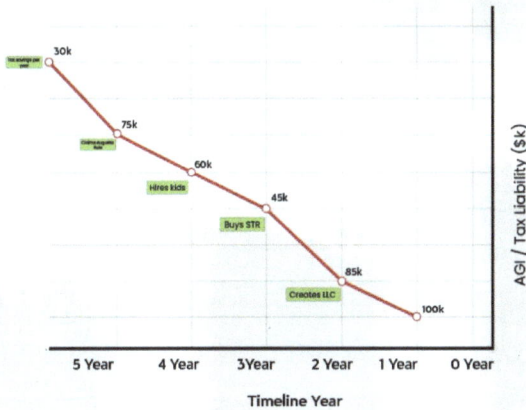

From Over-Taxed to Empowered

Within two years, Raj didn't just reduce his tax liability by over $100,000 annually, he changed his entire financial posture. He no longer feared tax season. He embraced it because now, he was in control.

He hadn't changed jobs. He hadn't taken on a massive risk. He had simply started thinking like a wealth builder.

That's what Route 1 is about.

If you're a W2 professional with high income, don't assume you're stuck. There are strategies available if you take the time to learn them, structure your actions, and surround yourself with professionals who know how to play the game.

Not all wealth builders are W2 employees. Some of you are already in business for yourselves. And while business ownership opens even more doors, it also brings complexity.

In the next chapter, we'll meet Priya, a business owner scaling her company, managing growth, and unlocking even deeper tax strategies available only to entrepreneurs.

Whether you're on Route 1 or considering Route 2, the destination is the same: economic freedom.

Let's turn the page and see how business owners build and protect lasting wealth.

Chapter 4: Route 2 – The Business Builder's Blueprint

Priya stood at the front of her warehouse, clipboard in hand, sweat on her brow, and a smile on her face. She had just landed her largest client yet, a national retail chain, and her logistics business was about to cross the $5 million revenue mark for the first time.

From the outside, it looked like Priya had "made it." She had built something from scratch: a company, a brand, a legacy. Internally, the stress was growing not just from managing cash flow or employees or customers but also from taxes.

Each year, her tax liability seemed to grow alongside her revenue. And worse, her CPA seemed more like a scorekeeper than a strategist. "You're doing great," he'd say, "but just be ready for a big tax bill." It felt like she was being penalized for success.

Priya had spent her entire career building something out of nothing. But she hadn't yet learned how to structure success so it lasted. That was about to change.

Beyond Building: Structuring for Wealth

Many first-generation business owners, like Priya, are builders by nature. They hustle, they grow, they solve problems daily. But they often forget that building a business is not the same as building wealth. In fact, without the right financial structure, a thriving business can become a tax trap.

Route 2 is for people like Priya. Entrepreneurs, self-employed professionals, and small business owners who want to transform income into generational wealth, and do so without losing half of it to the IRS.

Choosing the Right Entity: LLC vs S-Corp vs C-Corp

When Priya started her company, she formed an LLC. It was easy, flexible, and common. However, as her profits grew, she began hearing about S-Corps and C-Corps from other entrepreneurs.

Her research revealed a major insight: entity structure isn't one-size-fits-all.

Her LLC offered simplicity and pass-through taxation, but she was paying self-employment taxes on the entire profit.

Switching to an S-Corp allowed her to pay herself a "reasonable salary" and take the remaining profit as a distribution, which wasn't subject to payroll taxes.

A C-Corp, while taxed separately, opened doors for fringe benefits and potential lower tax rates on retained earnings, ideal for reinvesting in growth.

Priya worked with a tax strategist to restructure her operations and filed for S-Corp election retroactively. That single move saved her over $30,000 in payroll taxes in the first year.

Section 179 and Bonus Depreciation

Priya also upgraded her delivery fleet. Instead of simply expensing vehicles over five years, she learned about Section

179, which allowed her to immediately deduct the cost of qualifying equipment, including heavy vehicles, up to the annual IRS limit.

Even better, bonus depreciation let her write off 100% of the remaining value. By combining both strategies, she reduced her taxable income by over $200,000, legally and strategically.

Hiring Her Kids and Leveraging the Augusta Rule

Priya had two teenage children who often helped around the office. Instead of treating their help informally, she began paying them a salary through her business.

The IRS allows business owners to pay their children for real work performed, and if structured properly, this income is taxed at a much lower rate (often 0% up to the standard deduction limit). The kids used part of the income to fund Roth IRAs, while the rest went toward savings and college costs.

She also utilized the Augusta Rule. Her business paid her personally to rent their home for quarterly team strategy days. Fourteen days a year, tax-free rental income, directly into her household.

MERP: Medical Expense Reimbursement Plans

As a business owner, Priya could set up a Medical Expense Reimbursement Plan (MERP) that allowed her company to reimburse her family for out-of-pocket medical expenses.

This meant pre-tax dollars were now covering deductibles, prescriptions, and more, an immediate and tangible form of savings that W2 employees rarely access.

Life Insurance as a Business Tool

Instead of buying term insurance personally, Priya's business funded a permanent life insurance policy on her. Properly structured, the business paid the premiums, the policy built cash value that she could borrow against, and it created an exit strategy through retirement or succession planning.

This wasn't just protection. It was leverage. A place to store capital, access it tax-free, and ensure a smooth business transition in the future.

Equipment and Vehicle Deductions

Priya also learned how to document usage, log mileage, and classify equipment to maximize deductions.

Rather than buying equipment outright from personal accounts, she financed them through the business, deducted the full value (thanks to depreciation), and kept her cash flowing.

Retirement Planning Like a CEO

W2 employees have IRAs and 401(k)s. However, Priya, as a business owner, could establish a Solo 401(k) or a Defined Benefit Plan, allowing her to contribute six figures annually, all tax-deferred.

In one year, she moved over $120,000 into retirement accounts while dramatically lowering her AGI. Not only did she save on taxes today, but she also created future wealth that would grow without tax drag.

Cost Segregation for Business-Owned Property

When Priya bought a small office building, her CPA initially depreciated it over 39 years. But a cost segregation study changed everything.

Instead of slowly depreciating the whole property, the study broke it into components, such as flooring, lighting, and plumbing, which could be depreciated faster. This created $150,000 in accelerated depreciation, allowing her to reinvest more cash into the business.

Charitable Strategies That Pay Dividends

Priya was also philanthropic. By setting up a Donor-Advised Fund, she was able to donate appreciated stock, get a full deduction, and still control when and how the money was distributed to charities.

She also explored charitable remainder trusts and real estate donations, creating legacy impact while receiving immediate tax relief.

The Business Owner's Shift

Priya didn't have to become a tax attorney to lower her liability. She just had to start thinking like a strategist.

She realized that success wasn't just in top-line revenue, but in bottom-line preservation. That the business she built with sweat and sacrifice could also build wealth for herself, her children, and the causes she cared about.

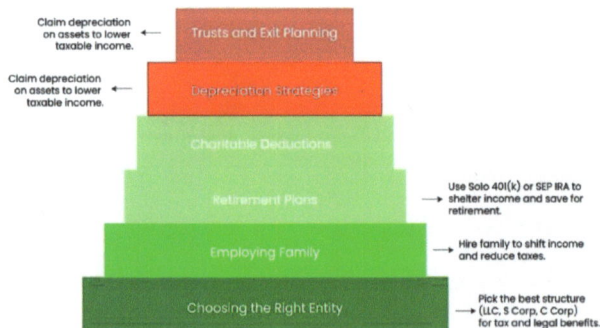

Business Structure Optimization Pyramid

With the right structure, guidance, and intent, Priya didn't just become a business owner. She became a wealth architect.

Earning and saving money is just the beginning. The next phase of the journey is protecting it. In the next chapter, we'll dive into the often-overlooked tools of wealth preservation: estate planning, trusts, wills, and asset protection.

The point isn't just to build wealth; it's to ensure it never gets lost.

Let's talk about how to leave a legacy, not just a balance sheet.

PART III:

Turning Taxes

Into Wealth –

Advanced Plays

Chapter 5: Hidden Gems in the Tax Code

Most people think of the tax code as a set of rules meant to extract money. But for those who take the time to look deeper, it reveals something surprising: it's also a roadmap filled with powerful incentives. These are not loopholes. They are intentional tools, planted by lawmakers to encourage investment, innovation, and social contribution.

After structuring income and protecting business profits, the next level is learning to leverage what I call the "hidden gems" of the tax code. These are advanced but accessible strategies that allow you to not only reduce taxes dramatically but also invest in meaningful, often high-impact areas.

Let's explore how these tools work and how people just like you are using them to reshape their financial future.

Timing is Everything: Section 461

In the world of taxation, when you recognize a loss, it matters just as much as the loss itself.

Under Section 461, certain losses can be accelerated to offset current-year income, even if the actual cash expense hasn't hit yet. This provision can be a game-changer for high-income earners who have passive losses or heavy investments in real estate or energy.

Take Ravi, a physician with a side real estate portfolio. In one year, his properties faced an unplanned capital expense, and he opted to apply Section 461 to pull forward certain deferred losses. That one strategic election wiped out over $200,000 in taxable income, reducing his tax burden by nearly $70,000.

This isn't everyday tax planning. It's high-level chess. But the move is legal, proven, and powerful when used under guidance.

1031 Exchange: Swapping, Not Selling

Real estate has always been a favorite for tax strategists, and Section 1031 is a big reason why.

According to IRS SOI (Statistics of Income) data, 1031 exchanges deferred over $100 billion in taxable gains in 2021 alone.

And a Deloitte survey found that 63% of high-income real estate investors use 1031 exchanges regularly.

A 1031 exchange allows you to sell one investment property and roll the profits into another, without triggering capital gains tax, as long as specific rules and timelines are met.

If you've ever wondered how large investors build entire portfolios without cashing out and getting crushed by taxes, this is how they do it.

Let's say you bought a duplex five years ago, and it's valued at $300,000. Instead of selling and losing 20–30% to taxes, you can "exchange" it for a new property and keep all your gains invested. Over time, you can do this again and again, compounding your real estate equity while deferring taxes until you're ready, or pass the assets on with a stepped-up basis at death, eliminating the tax altogether.

This is how wealth gets passed, not taxed.

Solar Investment Credits: Green Money

The government wants you to go solar, and it's willing to pay you for it.

The Investment Tax Credit (ITC) allows investors to deduct up to 30% of the cost of a solar energy system from their federal taxes. This applies not just to homeowners, but also to business owners and even passive investors who fund solar projects.

Priya, from our previous chapter, partnered with a clean energy syndicate. She invested $100,000 into a commercial solar installation and claimed $30,000 as a direct tax credit, not a deduction, but a dollar-for-dollar credit. On top of that, she qualified for bonus depreciation on the investment, further lowering her AGI.

These investments aren't just good for the planet. They're smart, asset-backed vehicles that generate income and equity while cutting your tax bill in half.

Tribal Tax Credits: Investing in Sovereignty

Another rarely discussed opportunity comes in the form of Tribal Tax Credits, offered through partnerships with Native American economic development zones.

A 2022 GAO report noted that for every $1 invested in tribal NMTC projects, investors receive an average return of $1.39 through credits and incentives.

These programs offer incentives, often in the form of 1:1 or better tax credits, for investing in businesses, infrastructure, or services within tribal lands.

For example, a $100,000 investment might generate a $100,000 credit against federal taxes, depending on the structure. The details can be complex, but the opportunity is enormous, both financially and socially. You're not just reducing taxes; you're helping build schools, hospitals, and jobs in underserved areas.

Mobile Home & Medical Device Donations: High-Multiplier Deductions

Sometimes, the biggest returns come from giving rather than investing.

High-impact donation programs exist that allow individuals to donate items like refurbished mobile homes or FDA-cleared medical devices to nonprofits, usually clinics, mobile care units, or shelters. These donations often qualify for enhanced deductions, where your appraised value can be 5x to 10x your cost basis.

For example, if you invest $20,000 in a refurbished mobile unit, you might receive a $100,000 charitable deduction. With proper documentation and an IRS-compliant appraisal, you could apply this deduction to up to 50% of your AGI in a given year.

The tax impact is significant, but more than that, the social return is extraordinary.

50% AGI Deduction Planning

This is where things get strategic. The IRS allows most individuals to deduct up to 60% of their AGI for cash donations (50% in some cases, depending on the entity receiving the donation).

According to Fidelity Charitable's 2023 report, donors who combine Donor-Advised Funds with non-cash gifts receive, on average, 24% more in tax savings than cash-only donors.

Let's say you make $400,000 this year. You could potentially deduct $200,000 through charitable giving, especially when leveraging high-multiplier strategies like mobile home or device donations.

Pair this with smart timing, and you could eliminate your federal tax liability altogether. That's the kind of outcome that turns taxes from a liability into a legacy tool.

Leveraging Bank Funds to Maximise Benefits

Finally, one of the most overlooked, but most powerful, concepts is using other people's money to fund these tax-advantaged investments.

You might invest $100,000 of borrowed funds into an oil and gas project, a solar development, or even a charitable structure that yields credits. The deduction or credit you receive can often far exceed the cost of borrowing, especially if the loan is interest-only or structured via a private lender or HELOC.

This is where strategy becomes synergy: you're using debt to fund tax savings, which then frees up capital to reinvest or accelerate other goals. The wealthy have done this for decades. Now, you can too.

Hidden No More

The tax code wasn't designed to punish wealth; it was designed to shape behavior. If you understand what behaviors are rewarded, you can align your goals accordingly.

Whether it's funding solar energy, supporting tribal communities, giving generously, or timing your losses with precision, the strategies in this chapter are not reserved for billionaires. They're available to anyone willing to study the rules, take action, and build a team that knows how to execute.

Now that we've covered how to earn and save strategically, it's time to turn to preservation. Because what's the point of building a castle if it can be taken from you?

In the next chapter, we'll explore the essential legal structures that protect your wealth, trusts, wills, asset protection strategies, and international planning, so that no court, creditor, or chaos can tear down what you've built.

Let's fortify your financial future.

Chapter 6: Insurance as an Investment Engine

Most people hear the word "life insurance" and think about death. A payout. A worst-case scenario.

But that limited view misses one of the most powerful tools in the wealth-building arsenal. When used strategically, life insurance becomes more than a safety net; it becomes a living asset, a private bank, and a generational wealth engine.

After my health scare, I knew I needed life insurance for protection. What I didn't know then, and what most people still don't, is how the wealthy have used insurance not just to protect income, but to store capital, shield assets, fund investments, and pass on legacy wealth tax-free.

Let's pull back the curtain on how life insurance can be an investment vehicle, a tax haven, and a blueprint for financial continuity.

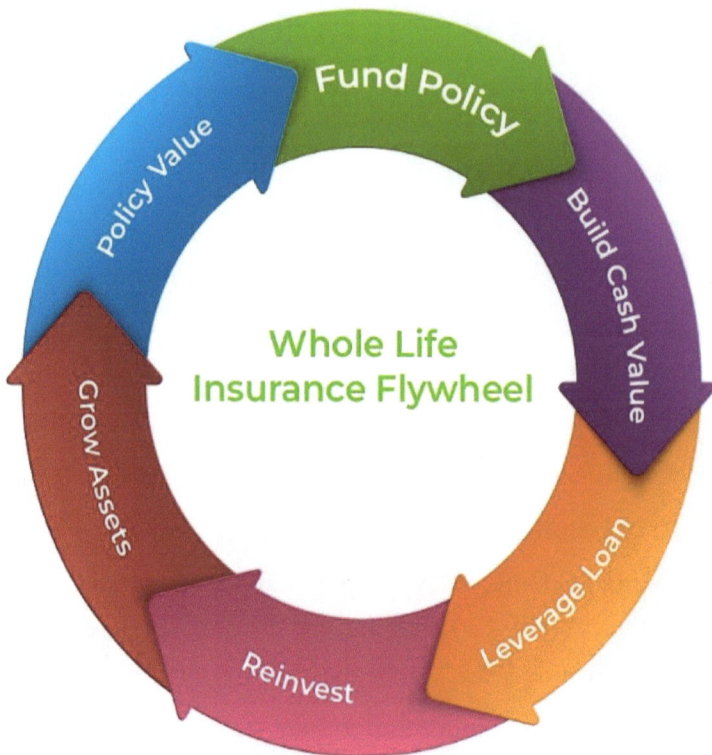

Whole Life Insurance Flywheel

Fund Policy → Build Cash Value → Leverage Loan → Reinvest → Grow Assets → Policy Value

Rethinking Insurance: Not a Bill, But a Bank

Traditional term insurance is like renting an apartment; it protects you, but builds nothing. It's affordable, straightforward, and expires. It's not an asset. It's a hedge.

However, Whole Life or Indexed Universal Life (IUL) policies operate differently. These are permanent policies with a cash value component that grows over time, often tax-deferred. Unlike retirement accounts, the cash inside a life insurance policy can be accessed tax-free via policy loans, without age restrictions, income limits, or penalties.

This is what's meant by "becoming your own bank."

Instead of withdrawing money and triggering a taxable event, you borrow against your own policy. The policy continues to earn interest and dividends as if the full amount were untouched, while you use the borrowed capital to fund investments, pay off high-interest debt, or support your business.

Consider this: the policy earns 5% compound growth, you borrow at 3%, and reinvest into a real estate deal earning 12%. That's positive arbitrage, liquidity control, and asset protection, all in one move.

Case Study: Becoming the Bank

Meet Arjun, a 38-year-old high-income sales executive. After maxing out his 401(k), Roth conversions, and real estate portfolio, he opened a $1M whole life policy with annual premiums of $50,000 for 10 years.

By year 6, his policy had over $250,000 in cash value. Instead of withdrawing money from his brokerage account to fund a real estate syndication, he borrowed money from his life insurance, which was tax-free.

- He still earned annual dividends of $250K, which are included in the policy.
- His investment earned 11% that year.
- He paid just 3% interest on the loan from the insurance carrier.

This is what banks do. They lend at higher rates than they borrow, and keep the spread. With life insurance, you can do the same, safely and legally.

Premium Financing: The Ultra-High-Net-Worth Strategy

For those with multi-million-dollar estates, premium financing offers a way to supercharge this model.

Here's how it works:

- Instead of paying massive premiums out of pocket, the individual uses a bank loan to fund the policy.
- The policy's growing cash value serves as collateral, and interest is paid annually (often at favorable rates).
- Upon death, the loan is repaid from the death benefit, and the remaining amount passes tax-free to beneficiaries.

This strategy is particularly effective for business owners or investors who want to preserve liquidity for operations while locking in large-scale, leveraged legacy wealth.

According to LIMRA, nearly 40% of ultra-high-net-worth individuals in the U.S. use some form of premium-financed life insurance to supplement estate planning or executive compensation.

Trust + Insurance = Legacy Without Probate or Taxes

One of the biggest benefits of permanent life insurance is how cleanly it passes to heirs, outside of probate, and often outside of estate tax exposure.

The secret? Irrevocable Life Insurance Trusts (ILITs).

When a life insurance policy is owned by a properly structured ILIT:

- The death benefit is excluded from your taxable estate.
- Heirs receive the proceeds quickly, without court involvement.

- The trust can include instructions for staggered disbursements, education funding, or generation-skipping gifts.

This strategy is vital in light of the 2026 sunset of the current estate tax exemption. With the exemption potentially dropping from over $13M to ~$7M per individual, many affluent families could suddenly find themselves exposed to estate taxes of 40% or more.

Smart families are using life insurance, inside trusts, to pre-fund those taxes or replace assets gifted to charity or heirs, tax-efficiently.

Business Continuity: The Ultimate Safety Net

For business owners, life insurance also plays a key role in succession planning.

- Key-person insurance ensures the company has liquidity if a founder or executive dies.
- Buy-sell agreements funded by insurance provide the cash to buy out a deceased partner's shares, keeping ownership within the company or family.

- Executive bonus plans (Section 162) allow companies to use life insurance as a retention tool, creating golden handcuffs and long-term incentive alignment.

Priya, from Chapter 4, implemented a cross-purchase buy-sell agreement with her co-founder, funded by equal insurance policies. If either passed away, the survivor would have immediate cash to buy the other's shares at a pre-agreed value, with no debt, no dilution, and no confusion.

Bonus: Asset Protection, Privacy, and Flexibility

In most states, the cash value of life insurance is protected from creditors, making it a stealthy place to store wealth.

Additionally, insurance does not trigger capital gains or 1099 reporting, giving it unmatched privacy compared to brokerage accounts.

And unlike retirement accounts, there are no RMDs, no early withdrawal penalties, and no income phase-outs.

It's control without compromise, liquidity without penalty, and wealth building with protection.

Life insurance is not about death; it's about leverage.

It's about putting your dollars to work in multiple directions at once:

- Earning interest
- Growing tax-deferred
- Protecting family
- Funding investments
- Securing legacy

Whether you're a W2 professional, business owner, or investor, this tool can become a cornerstone of your wealth plan when used wisely.

Don't wait until you "need" insurance. Use it while you're strong, healthy, and strategic. The future you will thank you.

Now that you've learned how to grow and leverage your wealth, it's time to shield it.

In the next chapter, we'll dive into asset protection: domestic and offshore trusts, international banking, laddering strategies, and how to safeguard everything you've built from lawsuits, taxation, and life's curveballs.

Because freedom is meaningless without security. Let's build your financial fortress.

PART IV:

Protect What You Build

Chapter 7: Estate Planning for Legacy and Protection

There's a quiet countdown happening in the background of your financial life. Most people don't hear it. But those who do are already preparing.

In recent years, federal estate tax laws have been historically generous, with exemption levels exceeding $13 million per individual (over $26 million per couple). But these laws are not permanent. Changes to tax policy are often driven by shifting political priorities, and many experts believe a reset is on the horizon.

Whether or not the current exemption is reduced, potentially to around $6–7 million per person in the coming years, the ianmplications for high-net-worth families are clear: now is the time to get proactive.

Imagine building a $10 million estate through real estate, business ownership, investments, and insurance. If exemption levels drop and you haven't planned properly, millions could be exposed to estate taxes, eroding what you intended to leave behind.

This chapter is about making sure that doesn't happen. Estate planning isn't about death, it's about designing the transfer of your life's work with intention, clarity, and control.

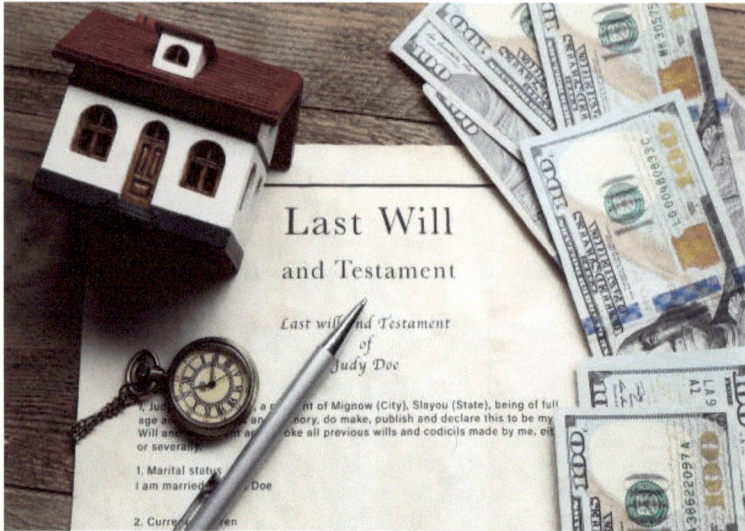

Why Estate Planning Is Urgent Now

A surprising number of high-income earners, and even business owners, think estate planning is something to do "later." The truth? Waiting could be the most expensive mistake of your life.

Without a proper estate plan:

- Your family could spend months or years in probate court.

- Assets might be taxed at 40% or more.
- Family disputes can erupt in the absence of legal clarity.
- Generational wealth may get stripped down at every transfer.

[A 2024 probate study by Trust & Will found that many Americans underestimate the costs and complexities of estate planning.](#) That's not just risky, it's irresponsible. Estate planning isn't for the ultra-rich anymore. If you own a home, a business, or a life insurance policy, you need a plan.

And with the 2026 exemption cliff approaching, there's never been a better time to act.

Step One: Living Trusts and Wills

A revocable living trust is the foundation of a modern estate plan. It allows you to:

- Avoid probate
- Keep your affairs private
- Maintain control over your assets during your lifetime
- Name clear beneficiaries for a smooth transition

Unlike a will, which becomes public record and requires court approval, a trust ensures seamless transfer of assets, often within weeks, not months.

But while living trusts help with administration and privacy, they don't offer estate tax protection. For that, you need to explore irrevocable trusts.

The Power of Irrevocable Trusts

An irrevocable trust removes assets from your personal estate. You no longer "own" the assets in the eyes of the IRS, which means they are no longer subject to estate tax.

Some of the most common types include:

- **ILITs (Irrevocable Life Insurance Trusts):** Hold large life insurance policies outside your estate, so the death benefit passes tax-free.
- **SLATs (Spousal Lifetime Access Trusts):** One spouse creates a trust for the benefit of the other, using today's high exemption before it disappears.
- **GRATs (Grantor Retained Annuity Trusts):** Transfer appreciating assets (like company shares) while minimizing gift tax impact.

These aren't just abstract tools. They are used by real families every day to shield tens of millions in assets, legally and permanently.

Layered Trust Strategies: Bulletproofing Your Estate

Smart estate planning uses layers of trust structures to build a fortress of protection. Here's how a layered plan might look:

- A **revocable trust** manages day-to-day assets.
- An **ILIT** holds life insurance and reduces estate tax exposure.
- A **dynasty trust** creates multigenerational wealth transfer.

- A **foreign trust** adds international asset protection and tax minimization.

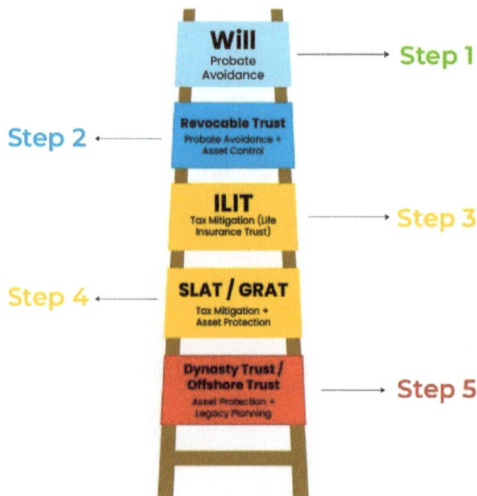

Estate Planning Ladder

This strategy isn't just for billionaires. Anyone with a net worth of $5 million or more should be exploring multi-tiered trust frameworks to avoid the 2026 trap.

Family Limited Partnerships (FLPs): Control with Tax Discounts

Family Limited Partnerships are powerful tools that allow you to:

- Maintain control of your assets
- Shift economic value to heirs
- Apply valuation discounts of 20–40%

Here's how it works:

1. You contribute business interests, real estate, or investments to an FLP.
2. You retain voting control while gifting non-voting shares to your children or a trust.

3. Because these shares are "minority interests" without market liquidity, the IRS allows you to value them at a discount.

That means you can gift $10 million in value while using only $6 million of your lifetime exemption. FLPs are particularly useful for business succession, property portfolios, and structured generational wealth transfer.

Charitable Remainder Trusts (CRTs): Give and Receive

What if you could avoid capital gains, get an immediate tax deduction, receive income for life, and leave a legacy?

That's the promise of the Charitable Remainder Trust.

You donate an appreciated asset (like stock or real estate) into the CRT. The trust sells the asset tax-free, reinvests it, and pays you or your spouse an income stream. After your lifetime, the remainder goes to a qualified charity.

This strategy works beautifully for:

- Reducing AGI in high-income years
- Unlocking gains without tax hits
- Supporting causes that align with your values

Bonus: You can pair a CRT with a Wealth Replacement Trust, a life insurance trust that passes an equivalent amount tax-free to your heirs, replacing what was gifted to charity.

Dynasty Trusts: Legacy That Lasts Forever

Most people plan for one generation. The ultra-wealthy plan for five.

Dynasty trusts are long-term irrevocable trusts designed to last for hundreds of years. Their benefits include:

- Avoiding estate tax at every generational transfer
- Shielding wealth from creditors, lawsuits, and divorce
- Creating structured disbursements over time
- Enabling values-based wealth transfer through education, home ownership, or philanthropy triggers

You can even appoint a Private Trust Company, a family-run board, to oversee the assets, replacing banks or outside trustees.

States like Nevada, South Dakota, and Wyoming allow dynasty trusts with no rule against perpetuity, making them ideal for long-term planning.

International Planning: Offshore Trusts and Jurisdictional Strategy

In a global world, risk can come from anywhere: economic instability, legal disputes, even political shifts. That's why many families turn to offshore structures for diversification and asset protection.

Jurisdictions like:

- **Cook Islands**
- **Nevis**
- **Switzerland**
- **Singapore**

...offer ironclad trust protection, financial privacy, and legal separation from U.S. courts. Properly structured, an offshore trust:

- Keeps assets beyond the reach of U.S. litigation
- Provides currency diversification
- May enable tax deferral or estate exclusion (when paired with U.S. compliance)

These strategies must be done with expert legal and tax guidance to remain fully compliant with U.S. law, but they are 100% legal when executed properly.

What To Do Now – The 2026 Checklist

Here's your actionable checklist to prepare before the sunset:

- ✓ Calculate your net worth including property, businesses, insurance, and retirement.
- ✓ Meet with a qualified estate attorney and a tax strategist.
- ✓ Use your exemption now by gifting into irrevocable trusts.
- ✓ Transfer appreciating assets out of your estate.
- ✓ Explore FLPs, SLATs, ILITs, and other layered trust models.
- ✓ Use valuation discounts when gifting.
- ✓ Consider charitable giving strategies like CRTs or DAFs.
- ✓ Set up or update your will, living trust, power of attorney, and healthcare proxy.
- ✓ Review life insurance ownership to avoid unintended estate inclusion.

✓ Evaluate international options for privacy and protection.

Remember: The clock isn't slowing down. The longer you wait, the fewer options you have.

Next Chapter: Invest in Your Future – Building Wealth with Intention

Now that we've addressed how to protect what you've built and how to transfer it wisely, it's time to shift focus, toward growth.

In the next chapter, we'll explore how to actively invest in your future using smart, diversified, and tax-advantaged strategies. From real estate and heavy equipment to cutting-edge AI tools and professional wealth management, you'll learn how to make your money work as hard as you do.

Because protecting your wealth is just one side of the coin, the other is multiplying it with purpose and precision.

Chapter 8: Invest in your Future

Legacy isn't just about what you leave behind, it's about how you live forward. Once you've built a structure to protect your wealth, the next step is growth. True wealth isn't just preserved, it's multiplied. Whether you're earning a strong salary, running a thriving business, or just beginning to explore the possibilities of financial independence, investing is the path forward. But not all investments are created equal, and not all strategies are designed with tax efficiency, long-term growth, or protection in mind.

The smartest investors don't just chase returns. They think in systems. They prioritize longevity over excitement, structure over speculation, and alignment over speed. In this chapter, we will unpack the strategies that help high-income individuals and savvy professionals invest wisely, tax-efficiently, and purposefully. We'll cover diversification, tax-advantaged investment vehicles, asset classes like real estate and heavy equipment, the use of artificial intelligence in wealth management, and why a professional advisory team is indispensable.

The Art and Purpose of Diversification

Diversification is often misunderstood as simply "not putting all your eggs in one basket." While technically true, the philosophy runs deeper. Diversification is about strategically allocating your capital across different asset classes, risk levels, and time horizons so that your portfolio is resilient against shocks, economic, geopolitical, or personal.

Most high-income professionals and business owners are overexposed to either their primary income source or a single investment category. A successful software engineer might be heavily weighted in tech stocks. A business owner might pour everything back into their company. But concentration breeds vulnerability. Diversification is your insurance against the unknown.

The most resilient portfolios include a mix of:

- Cash-flowing assets like rental properties or dividend stocks
- Long-term growth vehicles like equity index funds or private equity
- Inflation hedges like real estate and commodities
- Defensive assets like municipal bonds and treasury securities
- Liquid funds for emergencies or short-term opportunities

Diversification isn't about playing defense; it's about building a portfolio that performs well in various economic environments. And as you'll see, some investments do more than just grow your wealth, they shield it from taxes.

Why Tax-Advantaged Investing is a Superpower

The tax code isn't designed to punish the rich, it's designed to encourage specific behaviors. If you learn to read between the lines, you'll discover it's not just about how much you make, but how you make it and where you keep it.

Tax-advantaged investments are powerful because they allow you to keep more of your gains, compound faster, and reduce your effective tax rate.

Some of the most compelling vehicles include:

- **Municipal Bonds**: These provide tax-free interest income, especially attractive for those in high tax brackets. You're effectively lending money to state or local governments and receiving interest that the IRS doesn't touch.

- **Opportunity Zones**: By investing capital gains into designated underdeveloped areas, you can defer and potentially eliminate future taxes on those gains, depending on your holding period.

- **Oil and Gas Investments**: Through intangible drilling costs (IDCs), investors can deduct up to 100% of their investment in year one. These deductions offset active income, a unique benefit not found in most other investments.

- **Cost Segregation**: If you own real estate, a cost segregation study lets you front-load depreciation, dramatically reducing your taxable income in the early years of ownership. When combined with **bonus depreciation**, the tax savings can be significant.

These strategies don't just help with tax efficiency, they also promote more effective capital allocation. When the government incentivizes you to invest in real estate, energy, or infrastructure, it's because those sectors are vital to economic growth. By aligning your wealth-building with public policy, you gain access to outsized benefits.

Real Estate: The King of Wealth Vehicles

Real estate remains one of the most reliable and tax-advantaged investment classes. It offers consistent cash flow, appreciation, tax sheltering, and leverage, all in one package.

Whether it's a single-family rental, a multi-unit building, or a commercial property, real estate allows you to grow wealth while lowering your tax liability. The power lies in depreciation, a non-cash expense that reduces taxable income. When combined with cost segregation, you can accelerate that depreciation, taking deductions sooner and sheltering more income.

Add in 1031 exchanges, which allow you to defer capital gains tax by reinvesting proceeds into similar properties, and you have a compound growth engine that's hard to match.

And don't overlook short-term rentals. Properly managed, these can generate 2–3x the monthly income of long-term rentals. Even better? With material participation, you might qualify for tax benefits that offset W2 income, not just passive gains. For high-earning professionals, that's a rare loophole worth exploring.

Heavy Equipment Investments: A Hidden Tax Shield

One of the most overlooked opportunities for high-income individuals is investing in heavy equipment, trucks, trailers, excavators, cranes. These assets, often leased to logistics companies or construction firms, offer strong cash flow and massive upfront tax benefits.

Why? Because they qualify for Section 179 and bonus depreciation, allowing you to write off most or all of the asset's value in the first year, even if you financed the purchase. This creates a scenario where you're using the bank's money to generate cash flow and secure major tax write-offs.

Imagine this: You invest $200,000 into equipment that generates $4,000–5,000 per month in lease income, while simultaneously writing off $180,000 or more in year one. That's not just smart, that's transformative.

Some firms even offer fractional ownership models, where you can invest smaller amounts into large equipment pools and still receive proportional tax benefits and income streams.

The AI Advantage: Smart Tech for Smarter Investing

Artificial Intelligence is no longer a future concept, it's a current tool transforming how we manage money. AI-powered platforms can:

- Monitor your spending and flag inefficiencies
- Predict market trends and rebalance portfolios
- Alert you to tax-loss harvesting opportunities
- Help automate savings and investment contributions

Apps like Rocket Money analyze subscriptions and expenses to save you hundreds. Robo-advisors like Betterment or

Wealthfront help automate ETF investments. More advanced tools model real estate cash flows or use AI to spot arbitrage in niche asset classes.

However, AI works best alongside human judgment, not in place of it. Tech gives you data. A human advisor gives you context, foresight, and emotional discipline. Together, they form a powerful alliance.

The Value of Human Guidance: Your Personal Wealth Board

Behind every successful investor is a team. The ultra-wealthy don't make decisions in a vacuum. They lean on experts who challenge, support, and refine their strategies.

You need a personal board of directors, including:

- A **fiduciary financial advisor** to craft your roadmap
- A **tax strategist or CPA** to optimize your filings
- An **estate attorney** to protect your legacy
- A **real estate syndicator or broker** to uncover vetted deals
- An **insurance strategist** to structure wealth-preserving policies

Each plays a role. Each sees blind spots you don't. Together, they ensure you're not just making moves, but making the right ones.

When you're building a legacy, DIY isn't the answer. Collaboration is.

Invest With Vision, Not Just Metrics

As you build your portfolio, don't chase returns, chase alignment. Ask yourself:

- What do I want my life to look like in 10 years?
- How much time and effort am I willing to spend managing assets?
- Do I want monthly cash flow, long-term growth, or both?
- What values do I want my investments to reflect?

Your investment decisions should be extensions of your goals, not distractions from them. The best portfolios are personal. They're built with intention, not imitation.

Theory is powerful. But nothing reinforces strategy like seeing it in action.

Diversified Investment Portfolio Wheel

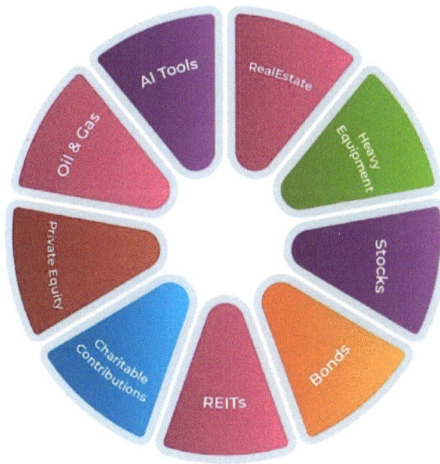

In the next chapter, we'll dive into real-world examples and case studies, from entrepreneurs designing their exit strategies, to families shielding their assets from lawsuits, to professionals using creative tax deferral and charitable giving. You'll see how high-income individuals and business owners across the country are applying the very strategies we've covered, building passive income, maximizing retirement accounts through SDIRAs and ROBS, and mastering Roth conversions.

This is where ideas meet impact. Let's bring it to life.

Chapter 9: Case Studies and Examples

Reading about strategy is one thing. Watching it transform someone's financial life is another. This chapter bridges the gap between theory and action, with real-life examples that reveal how powerful these tax-saving and wealth-building tools can be when used intentionally.

You'll meet professionals, business owners, and families who made bold decisions to protect, grow, and ultimately pass on their wealth. These aren't abstract models, they're reflections of what's possible when you approach your money with clarity, courage, and a game plan.

Let's begin with one of the biggest wealth events of all: the business exit.

Case Study 9.1: The Entrepreneur's Exit Strategy – Sarah's Phased Departure

Scenario:

Sarah, co-founder of RoboNav Solutions, had grown her AI-driven robotics company into a multimillion-dollar powerhouse. But after 15 years, she was ready to step back.

Challenge:

How can a founder sell her stake without triggering massive taxes or destabilizing the company?

Strategy Implemented:

Sarah structured a phased equity sell-down to a strategic acquirer, avoiding a one-time windfall. She incorporated an ESOP to retain key staff and set up a CLAT, donating shares to reduce her estate. An installment sale agreement spread capital gains, and the charitable vehicle allowed her to give back while supporting her heirs.

Outcome:

Sarah exited with grace, preserved her legacy, and minimized taxes while benefiting causes she believed in.

Key Takeaways:

- An exit is not an event; it's a process.
- Charitable trusts and installment sales reduce tax impact.
- ESOPs ensure leadership continuity.

Case Study 9.2: Protecting Assets from Lawsuits – Mark's Real Estate Fortress

Scenario:

Mark, a commercial real estate developer, owned over 30 income-producing properties.

Challenge:

How to shield his portfolio from lawsuits, construction disputes, and liability?

Strategy Implemented:

He structured each property under a separate LLC and formed a DAPT. He also conducted cost segregation studies under Section 168 to accelerate depreciation on new developments, generating major tax deductions upfront. A $10M umbrella policy provided an additional safety net. He later structured mineral rights and oil & gas royalties through limited partnerships, placing ownership in trusts for asset protection and estate planning.

Outcome:

Despite facing lawsuits over tenant injuries and project delays, Mark's personal and business wealth remained intact.

Key Takeaways:

- Asset separation through LLCs limits liability.
- **Section 168 depreciation and cost segregation accelerate write-offs.**

- **Minerals and royalties offer passive income and legal insulation.**

Case Study 9.3: Minimizing Taxes Through Charitable Giving – Lisa's Legacy Planning

Scenario:

Lisa, a tech executive, wanted to offload appreciated stock while supporting education.

Challenge:

How to give generously without losing 30% to capital gains?

Strategy Implemented:

Lisa funded a DAF with appreciated stock, avoiding gains and claiming a deduction. She then set up a CRT for lifetime income and charitable legacy. Lisa also invested the CRT assets into REITs and energy-focused MLPs, generating regular distributions while maintaining liquidity and tax efficiency.

Outcome:

Lisa reduced her taxable income, increased giving capacity, and structured her retirement income wisely.

Key Takeaways:

- Donating appreciated assets avoids capital gains.
- **REITs and MLPs can provide steady income inside charitable vehicles.**
- DAFs and CRTs optimize giving timing and impact.

Case Study 9.4: Building Passive Income Through Real Estate – David's Escape Plan

Scenario:

David, a high-earning software engineer, was burned out and looking for stable cash flow.

Challenge:

How to transition from stocks to passive income without managing tenants?

Strategy Implemented:

David began buying single-family homes in Texas and Georgia using 30-year fixed loans. He applied cost segregation to each property to claim accelerated depreciation and lower his W-2 income. Later, he invested in apartment syndications and REITs for scale and liquidity.

Outcome:

David built $15,000/month in passive income. Thanks to cost segregation, his paper losses exceeded $100K per year, sheltering other income.

Key Takeaways:

- **Cost segregation accelerates depreciation under IRS rules (Section 168).**
- REITs and syndications offer hands-free exposure.
- Real estate complements equity portfolios with income and tax sheltering.

Case Study 9.5: Using SDIRA and ROBS – Emily's Unconventional Retirement Move

Scenario:

Emily wanted to use her IRA to invest in a robotics franchise and commercial space.

Challenge:

How to unlock retirement dollars without incurring penalties?

Strategy Implemented:

Emily created a Self-Directed IRA with checkbook control, allowing her to invest directly in startup equity and real estate. She used a ROBS strategy to roll her 401(k) into her new C-corporation and purchase shares with it, funding business growth.

Outcome:

Emily grew her net worth using tax-deferred capital, while maintaining full IRS compliance.

Key Takeaways:

- SDIRAs allow real estate, startup, and mineral investments.
- ROBS enables business funding from retirement funds.
- Legal compliance is critical in self-directed accounts.

Case Study 9.6: Deferring Taxes Through 1031 Exchanges – John's Legacy Portfolio

Scenario:

John wanted to sell a $5 million apartment complex with major appreciation.

Challenge:

How to upgrade properties without triggering taxes?

Strategy Implemented:

He executed a 1031 Exchange through a Qualified Intermediary, trading into two Class-A properties in Phoenix. He used cost segregation on the new properties for bonus depreciation, layering tax savings.

Outcome:

John deferred $2 million in gains, boosted income, and improved his portfolio's quality.

Key Takeaways:

- 1031 Exchanges defer capital gains.
- **Combining them with cost segregation compounds tax efficiency.**
- Strict timelines must be followed precisely.

Case Study 9.7: Roth Conversions – Maria's Lifetime Tax Planning

Scenario:

Maria, 45, predicted higher future tax brackets due to rising income.

Challenge:

How to reposition her retirement assets for tax-free growth?

Strategy Implemented:

She performed annual backdoor Roth contributions and used a partial Roth conversion during a sabbatical. She also reallocated a portion of her Roth IRA into private REITs and mineral royalties for long-term tax-free growth.

Outcome:

Maria's Roth IRA now holds $900K, growing tax-free and structured to pass to her heirs without taxes.

Diversified Investment

Name	Cost Seg	1031	DAF	CRT	SDIRA
Raj	✓	✓			
Priya			✓	✓	✓
David	✓		✓		✓
Lisa		✓		✓	

Key Takeaways:

- Roth conversions shine during low-income years.
- **Tax-free REIT and royalty income compounds faster in Roths.**
- Early planning leads to multi-decade benefits.

Summary Table: Strategies by Case

Strategy	Individual	Key Outcome
Phased Exit + CLAT	Sarah	Tax-efficient exit and charitable legacy
LLC Layering + DAPT + Depreciation	Mark	Lawsuit protection + major depreciation deductions
DAF + CRT + QCD + REITs	Lisa	Strategic giving + income with tax sheltering
Real Estate + Cost Seg + REITs	David	Passive income + aggressive tax deduction strategy
SDIRA + ROBS	Emily	Invested retirement in startups and real estate

1031 + Cost Seg	John	Deferred taxes + boosted depreciation post-upgrade
Roth Conversion + Alt Assets	Maria	Built a tax-free retirement nest egg with REITs/royalties

What if you could make an impact and create wealth-building advantages at the same time?

In the next chapter, we explore how establishing your own 501(c)(3), leveraging grant-writing, and supporting high-impact missions, from clean energy to education, can unlock tax efficiencies, legacy planning benefits, and long-term value.

It's time to multiply wealth through purpose.

Chapter 10: Non-Profits as Wealth Multipliers

There comes a time when wealth is no longer just about net worth, it's about net impact. When your financial freedom intersects with a deeper purpose, your dollars gain a different kind of power: the ability to create change. This chapter is about using that power strategically through nonprofit organizations.

For many, the idea of creating a nonprofit sound like a purely philanthropic act. And it is. But it's also a powerful wealth strategy, one that blends mission with method, compassion with calculation. Nonprofits can offer tax relief, estate planning advantages, community elevation, and family legacy benefits that few other tools can match.

Let's explore how building or supporting a nonprofit can become a multiplier in your wealth journey, not just for giving, but for growing and protecting wealth as well.

What This Chapter Covers

- How to create your own 501(c)(3) organization
- Understanding the mechanics of nonprofit funding, grants, and compliance

- Real-world applications: medical missions, scholarships, clean energy initiatives
- Using charitable contributions to legally reduce taxable income
- How family-run nonprofits can teach values, preserve legacy, and create intergenerational wealth alignment

The Motivation Behind Mission

When I began exploring nonprofits, I didn't come at it like a philanthropist. I came at it like a father who wanted to protect his wealth while creating meaning for the next generation. I saw wealthy families not just donating, but building structures that lived on, doing good while strategically saving on taxes and directing wealth where it mattered.

I realized: Why wait until I'm gone to have an impact?

Creating a nonprofit is like planting a seed that grows into both a legacy and a shield. It can fund causes you care about, employ your children, support your community, and qualify for substantial tax advantages, all while staying legally compliant.

Creating Your Own 501(c)(3): The Foundation of Impact

The most commonly used nonprofit structure in the U.S. is the 501(c)(3), named after the IRS code that governs tax-exempt charitable organizations. Creating one is more accessible than many people think.

Step-by-Step: How to Form a 501(c)(3)

1. **Define Your Mission**

   It needs to align with one of the IRS-approved charitable purposes: education, relief of the poor, scientific research, religion, animal welfare, and so on. Make this mission clear and compelling.

2. **Form a Nonprofit Corporation in Your State**

   File articles of incorporation with your Secretary of State, including your mission, board structure, and bylaws.

3. **Apply for an EIN**

   Just like any business, your nonprofit needs an Employer Identification Number from the IRS.

4. **File IRS Form 1023 or 1023-EZ**

This is the application for federal tax-exempt status. If your organization expects under $50,000/year in gross receipts for the first 3 years, you can use the streamlined Form 1023-EZ.

5. **Maintain Compliance**

File annual IRS Form 990 or 990-EZ, keep board meeting minutes, and follow your bylaws. Transparency is key.

Once approved, donations to your nonprofit become tax-deductible for donors, and that includes you.

Strategic Uses of Nonprofits: From Outreach to Offsets

Let's explore how nonprofits can be used beyond goodwill to support high-impact, high-efficiency financial planning.

Medical Missions or Health Outreach

If you're passionate about health or wellness, starting a nonprofit focused on medical aid, such as donating medical devices, organizing surgical camps, or supporting preventive care, can unlock incredible benefits.

- **Tax Benefit**: You can often deduct up to 50% of your Adjusted Gross Income (AGI) through donations.
- **Multiplication**: Some devices or services donated can qualify for 1:5 or even 1:10 write-offs depending on how they're appraised and deployed.

Clean Energy Projects

A nonprofit centered on solar energy education or access in underserved areas not only contributes to sustainability but may also align with tribal or green energy credits. In some cases, you can partner your nonprofit with for-profit ventures (with clear arms-length rules) to secure funding or grants.

Scholarships and Education Funds

Want to support education? You can create a nonprofit to issue scholarships to students based on merit, need, or interest areas, especially in fields like STEM, robotics, or the arts. You can even name the scholarship after a loved one, creating legacy and impact at once.

Grant Writing and Outside Funding: Think Bigger Than Your Bank Account

Many people think a nonprofit has to be self-funded. It doesn't.

Once your nonprofit is established, you can apply for grants from local, state, and federal agencies, as well as private foundations. There are literally billions of dollars in grant funding available each year, and much of it goes unclaimed.

For example:

- **Community Development Block Grants** (CDBGs) for local outreach
- **STEM Education Grants** from tech companies and educational bodies
- **Clean Energy Grants** from the Department of Energy
- **Health Access Grants** for underserved populations

A well-written grant proposal aligned with your mission can unlock hundreds of thousands of dollars, or more, without touching your personal assets.

Leveraging Nonprofits to Reduce Taxable Income

Beyond social good, nonprofits can significantly optimize your tax position. Strategic charitable giving, especially to your own 501(c)(3), can dramatically reduce your adjusted gross income (AGI) and even offset capital gains or estate taxes when structured correctly..

Impact + Benefit

Example: Donating Appreciated Assets

Let's say you have a highly appreciated stock or real estate asset. Instead of selling and realizing a massive capital gain, you donate it to your nonprofit.

- **Tax Benefit**: You avoid capital gains entirely.
- **Write-Off**: You deduct the full fair market value of the asset up to 30% (for securities) or 50% (for cash or ordinary assets) of your AGI.
- **Impact**: The nonprofit then sells the asset tax-free and uses the proceeds to fund its mission.

This method is especially effective when paired with wealth transfer strategies like Charitable Remainder Trusts or Donor-Advised Funds (DAFs), which let you retain some control over the assets and the giving timeline while still receiving the tax benefits upfront.

Qualified Charitable Distributions (QCDs)

For readers over age 70½ with traditional IRAs, QCDs allow you to transfer up to $100,000 per year directly from your IRA to a qualified charity. This satisfies your Required Minimum Distribution (RMD) and reduces your taxable income dollar for dollar, without increasing your AGI.

Teaching Values and Preserving Legacy

Establishing a family-run nonprofit also becomes a vehicle for more than just taxes, it becomes a legacy. Your children can serve on the board, participate in grantmaking decisions, and help direct community programs. This accomplishes three powerful goals:

1. **Instills Financial Literacy**: Board meetings and financial reviews expose the next generation to money management and impact investing.
2. **Aligns Family Values**: Instead of just inheriting wealth, they inherit a purpose-driven system that reflects what matters to you.
3. **Strengthens Family Bonds**: Joint philanthropic decision-making can create cohesion and unity among family members.

By involving your children or heirs in the operation of the nonprofit, you build a family culture of giving, stewardship, and community leadership, all while maintaining strategic control of assets.

Case Example: The Nair Family Scholarship Foundation

The Nairs were a first-generation immigrant couple who found financial success in healthcare and real estate. As their wealth grew, they wanted to support other immigrant students pursuing medicine.

They created a 501(c)(3) foundation focused on scholarships and mentorship. The foundation was funded through appreciated stocks, a portion of their real estate profits, and family donations.

- They hired their two college-age children to manage communications, events, and outreach, paying them reasonable salaries.
- The children learned nonprofit accounting, grant writing, and strategic planning, while also networking with professionals in medicine and law.
- Over time, the foundation grew into a $2 million endowment providing 10–15 scholarships annually, and the Nairs used it to teach legacy, service, and responsibility.

Tax benefit? Substantial. Family impact? Immeasurable.

Combining Impact with Innovation

As technology and finance continue to evolve, new tools are emerging that make nonprofit work even more scalable and efficient.

- **AI-powered grant discovery platforms** (e.g., Instrumentl, GrantStation) help automate finding and applying for funding.
- **Blockchain for transparency** in donation tracking builds trust among donors and increases funding potential.
- **Social entrepreneurship hybrids** (B Corps or nonprofit/for-profit partnerships) allow you to structure organizations that combine mission with margin.

Even traditional nonprofits can modernize operations through digital fundraising, virtual events, and online donor engagement, reducing costs and increasing reach.

Strategic Nonprofit Levers

Strategy	Benefit	Wealth Multiplier Impact
Create 501(c)(3)	Full tax-exemption + donation deductibility	Legal control of mission-aligned assets

Donate appreciated stock or real estate	Avoid capital gains + FMV deduction	Higher write-offs, lower AGI
Use DAFs or CRTs	Deferred or managed giving	Estate and income tax benefits
Employ children in nonprofit	Teach skills + reduce taxable income	Intergenerational wealth literacy
Apply for grants	Outside capital to scale impact	Preserves personal capital
Conduct QCDs from IRAs	Satisfy RMDs tax-free	Lowers taxable income in retirement
Run education, medical, or energy causes	Qualifies for impact grants + media coverage	Expands credibility and influence

Closing Thoughts: Making Wealth Matter

Nonprofits are not just a charitable footnote in a financial plan. They are multipliers of wealth, influence, and meaning. When structured correctly, they create a flywheel effect, amplifying your legacy, reducing your tax burden, engaging your family, and changing the world around you.

They let you write a different kind of story. One where your wealth doesn't just outlast you, but outlives you in the best way possible.

We've now explored how to build, protect, and give through your wealth. But what happens when it's time to pass the torch? In the next chapter, we'll step into the living room, not the boardroom, as we uncover how a single conversation with your family can shape generations.

We'll talk about how to teach your children the values behind the money, how to write a "family constitution" that outlines your vision, and how to leave more than assets, you'll leave clarity, confidence, and unity.

Let's make wealth a conversation, not a secret.

PART V:

Beyond the

Numbers – Your

Wealth Legacy

Chapter 11: The Family Meeting That Changed Everything

It wasn't in a lawyer's office or a boardroom. It happened around our dining table, on a quiet Sunday afternoon.

I had just finished explaining a trust I had set up, detailing how assets would flow, who the trustees were, and why certain choices were made. My wife, Pallavi, listened carefully, asking questions I had never imagined. My daughter Anushka looked curious but puzzled, while Ashank fiddled with a Rubik's Cube, tuning in and out. But when I paused and said, "This isn't just about money, it's about you all knowing what to do if I'm not here," everything changed.

That moment forced me to remember that this entire journey didn't start with money; it started with my heart stopping. Literally. Bradycardia attacks. My heart rate going to zero. Being revived. The pacemaker that still beats for me. I realized that if I could go in an instant, I had to make sure my family was protected, informed, and ready. That health crisis was my wake-up call to plan not just for wealth, but for clarity and peace of mind.

That meeting was the most important financial planning event of my life, not because we reviewed accounts, but because we initiated clarity, trust, and understanding. And I realized then that wealth, without conversation, can become a curse.

Why Families Fall Apart Over Wealth

In many affluent households, wealth is kept quiet. It's either "too complicated" or "not appropriate to talk about with kids." But the result of that silence is predictable: confusion, resentment, poor decision-making, and even legal battles after a parent passes.

According to a 2022 study by The Williams Group, over 70% of intergenerational wealth transfers fail. The reason? Lack of communication and trust. Not bad investments. Not bad estate plans. Just bad conversations, or none at all.

Your legacy is not just the assets you leave behind. It's the understanding, values, and clarity you equip your family with.

Making the Conversation Safe and Strategic

The "family meeting" doesn't have to be dramatic or formal. It can start simply:

"I want to make sure you're all taken care of, and I want you to understand why I've made the choices I have."

That statement alone can open the door. From there, the goal is to:

- Share your financial philosophy
- Explain the key structures (wills, trusts, insurance)
- Empower your spouse with knowledge of all accounts and advisors
- Set expectations around inheritance and responsibilities
- Introduce the idea of a *family constitution*

In our case, I didn't just talk, I shared exactly what I had put in place after my health scare:

• An Estate Plan, Trust, and Will so they would never be in limbo

• Life Insurance strategies: Term, Whole Life, and Indexed Universal Life to cover all needs

• An IRA to Roth Conversion Plan to reduce future tax burdens

• Investments specifically designed to reduce taxable income now and, in the future.

• Buying a business not just to build wealth, but to teach my children how to manage, lead, and think like owners

• Setting up a Non-Profit to direct proceeds from this very book to help others in need

• Investing in assets for legacy wealth, including crypto, to diversify and future-proof

• Coordinating all this with a Tax Planner and CPA to make sure nothing was missed and everything was integrated

I told them all of it. I wanted no secrets, no surprises. Just clarity.

Wealth Vulnerability Chart

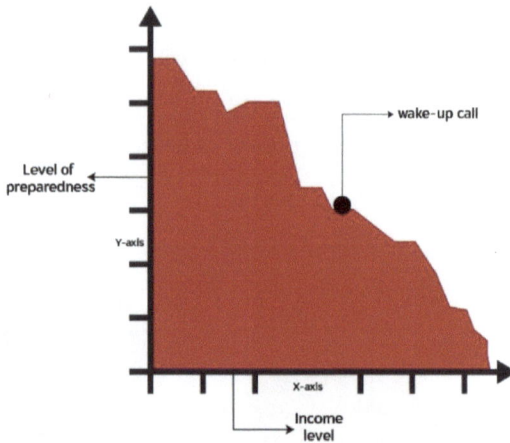

Teaching Your Kids About Wealth, Before They Inherit It

Children, especially in high-net-worth households, often grow up shielded from money discussions. The intent may be protection, but the result is usually unpreparedness.

If they've never budgeted, worked, or dealt with taxes, how can they be expected to manage six or seven figures one day?

You don't have to give them all the numbers. But give them the framework.

Teach them:

- The difference between assets and liabilities
- The basics of taxes and passive income
- How compounding works
- Why charitable giving matters
- What your values are around spending and saving

Consider using tools like:

- A **custodial Roth IRA** (for teenagers with earned income)
- **Allowance systems** tied to age-appropriate responsibilities
- Letting them manage a mock portfolio and discuss performance
- Bringing them to meetings with your financial advisor

For us, teaching our children to manage the business is one of the most important lessons. I didn't just want them to inherit wealth. I wanted them to understand how to create it, sustain it, and respect it.

Even one conversation a quarter can change their trajectory.

Creating a Family Constitution

A family constitution is not a legal document, it's a living guide that outlines your family's values, vision, and principles for how wealth should be used, protected, and grown.

What it can include:

- Your mission as a family (e.g., "To be generous stewards of our resources")
- Investment and giving principles
- Roles and responsibilities (e.g., who oversees trusts or foundations)
- Education and involvement criteria for future generations
- Guidelines for family business participation
- Succession planning philosophy

This document acts as a lighthouse, especially in emotionally charged moments, when someone passes, or a big decision must be made. It brings everyone back to shared values, not just shared blood.

You can write it yourself, with your spouse, or work with a family governance consultant. What matters is that it reflects your voice and is reviewed every couple of years with your family.

Writing Your "Letter of Wishes"

Beyond legal documentation, a Letter of Wishes is a deeply personal, non-binding letter you write to your trustees, heirs, or family members. It's your chance to speak directly, human-to-human, about what matters most.

In this letter, you can:

- Explain *why* you made certain estate planning decisions
- Share your hopes for how the wealth will be used
- Offer guidance on stewardship, relationships, or legacy
- Express personal messages to your spouse or children
- Outline your vision for any family foundation or business

It's one of the most powerful things you can leave behind, and something no lawyer can draft for you.

Empowering Your Spouse With Financial Clarity

In many households, especially traditional ones, one partner handles most financial decisions. But this leaves the other spouse vulnerable if something happens.

I realized, during my own health crisis, that Pallavi didn't know where our key documents were. She didn't know who our insurance agent was. Not because she couldn't understand it, she was simply never included.

That changed quickly.

Now, we do quarterly "check-ins." We walk through:

- Bank and investment accounts
- Life insurance policies
- Trust structures and beneficiaries
- Password managers and digital vaults
- Advisor contact info
- Healthcare and emergency plans

We even role-played: "If I were gone today, here's what you'd do first."

These are hard conversations, but they are the most loving ones.

The Emotional ROI of Transparency

When families talk openly about money, something unexpected happens. The tension drops.

Children feel trusted. Spouses feel empowered. Heirs feel included rather than controlled. And most importantly, you feel peace, knowing the plan isn't just written but understood.

Financial legacy without emotional preparation is like leaving someone a ship without teaching them to sail.

Start with one meeting. Set the tone. Invite questions. And revisit regularly.

Key Takeaways

- **Transparency is protection.** Don't leave your family guessing.
- **Start early, talk often.** Legacy isn't built in one conversation.
- **Documents are only as powerful as the understanding behind them.**
- **Include your family.** This is their story too.
- **Empower, don't just provide.** Education is part of the inheritance.

You've built the strategies. You've protected your legacy. You've brought your family into the fold. But now it's time to ask the deeper question: What's it all for?

In the next and final chapter, we go beyond spreadsheets and tax codes to explore the real meaning of wealth, freedom of time, flexibility, peace of mind, and the ability to reinvest in what matters most. Whether that's nurturing your health, deepening your relationships, giving back to causes you care about, or simply living without financial fear, economic freedom is the destination all of this effort has been pointing toward.

Let's talk about how to live free, not just plan well.

Chapter 12: Economic Freedom – Not Just About You

Most people chase money. But few stop to ask why.

Why do we wake up before sunrise, race through back-to-back meetings, manage the chaos of growing careers or businesses, only to rinse and repeat the next day? Why do we sacrifice health, sleep, time with our children, and inner peace just to earn more?

The answer lies in a misunderstanding, not of money, but of freedom.

What if the goal isn't to accumulate numbers in an account, but to reclaim your life, your time, your energy, your peace of mind? What if true wealth isn't about status or power, but about choice?

That's what economic freedom really is. The ability to choose your day, your priorities, your purpose. The freedom to stop trading time for money, to walk away from unnecessary stress, to show up fully for the people and passions that matter most.

And here's the truth: economic freedom isn't just about you. It's about everyone you touch. Your family. Your community. The world you leave behind. It's not a solo journey, it's a ripple effect. When you gain control over your finances, you free up the space to contribute more deeply to the world around you.

What Does Economic Freedom Really Mean?

Most financial books end with a number, a net worth target, a portfolio benchmark, or a retirement milestone. This book ends with a question:

What are you really building all this for?

Economic freedom isn't about retiring at 40 or sipping drinks on a beach (though you could). It's about living each day on your own terms. It's the ability to say "yes" to what matters and "no" to what doesn't, without worrying about the financial fallout.

It's about waking up without dread. Being present with your children instead of distracted by bills. Choosing meaningful work over mandatory work. Donating generously. Traveling without debt. Living a life that reflects your values.

It's not about how much you have. It's about how much control you have over your life.

Time, Flexibility, and Peace of Mind

Money alone doesn't bring peace of mind. But financial systems, habits, and structures can.

When you've built multiple income streams, when your tax strategies are dialed in, when your insurance and estate plans are in place, you sleep better. You stop bracing for impact every time there's a market dip, an emergency, or a tax bill.

Flexibility is the new luxury. Can you take three months off to care for a sick parent? Can you leave a toxic job without financial panic? Can you downshift from a 60-hour week to a 30-hour week and still maintain your lifestyle?

Peace of mind doesn't come from working harder. It comes from planning smarter. From having a strategy. From not being at the mercy of every economic fluctuation. It comes from owning your life, instead of being owned by your obligations.

Reinvesting in What Matters

Once the basics are handled, once your cash flow is solid, your taxes are minimized, your legacy is protected, it's time to reinvest in the only assets that truly appreciate with time: your relationships, your health, your purpose.

Family

Economic freedom means showing up for your loved ones. Not just with money, but with time, energy, and attention. It means being there for your kids' milestones, your spouse's dreams, your parents' needs. It means breaking generational cycles of stress and survival and rewriting a new narrative of strength, security, and support.

Health

All the wealth in the world means nothing if your body breaks down. Use your freedom to invest in nutrition, movement, rest, and mental health. Go to therapy. Meditate. Take vacations that actually recharge you. Eat food that nourishes you. Exercise not to impress others, but to honor the vessel that carries you through life.

Freedom isn't just financial, it's physical, emotional, and spiritual too.

Spirituality and Purpose

Whether you're religious, spiritual, or just introspective, economic freedom gives you the bandwidth to explore the deeper meaning of your life. Volunteer. Mentor. Start a nonprofit. Write a book. Build a school. Plant trees. Launch a foundation. Support the causes that make your heart beat faster.

Freedom is not just the absence of constraint, it's the presence of purpose.

A New Definition of Wealth

So far in this book, we've talked about:

- Strategic tax optimization
- Smart investing
- Legacy and estate planning
- Insurance and asset protection
- Passive income and business structuring

But none of it matters unless it leads somewhere bigger. True wealth is not just financial capital, it's also relational capital, spiritual capital, time capital. It's the ability to make choices from abundance, not fear.

Let's redefine wealth, not as how much you earn, but as how deeply you live.

- Do you feel safe?
- Do you feel healthy?
- Do you feel connected?
- Do you feel in control of your time?
- Do you feel free?

Those are your real metrics.

Who You Become Along the Way

Economic freedom changes your bank account. But more importantly, it changes your identity.

You become a better steward. A better parent. A better spouse. A more grounded version of yourself.

It makes you generous, not anxious. Strategic, not reactive. It helps you play offense in life instead of just defense. You begin to respond instead of merely react. You begin to lead, not just follow.

The journey to wealth is really the journey to yourself. Every dollar you save, every plan you create, every asset you protect, it all reflects a choice to honor your values and your vision.

Give Yourself Permission

If you're still early in your career, start with intention. You don't need to wait until you "make it" to begin thinking like someone who already has. Small decisions, automating savings, learning tax basics, living below your means, compound powerfully over time.

If you're already a high-income earner, optimize what you've built. Don't let the default path dictate your future. Use the strategies in this book to unlock tax efficiency, build legacy structures, and create income that works for you.

If you're in transition, changing careers, raising children, caring for aging parents, know that freedom is still possible. It just requires a little more creativity, and a lot more clarity.

No matter where you are, you are not behind. You are right on time. But only if you start now.

This Journey Is Bigger Than You

One day, your children will ask how you did it.

How you stayed calm during a recession. How you provided options when others had none. How you funded their dreams without fear. How you left something that lasted longer than you.

That is your legacy.

Economic freedom isn't about becoming rich. It's about becoming resilient. It's about making decisions that outlive you. It's about building something so solid that your children don't inherit just your money, they inherit your mindset.

You don't need to be perfect. You just need to be intentional. Freedom doesn't come all at once. It comes from one smart decision after another, in alignment with what you value most.

So start now.

Invest in yourself.

Build systems that last.

Teach your children how to think, not just what to own.

Live like your time matters.

Give like your legacy depends on it.

And when in doubt, remember:

You don't have to know everything.

You just have to know what matters.

And protect it.

From Strategy to Stewardship

At this point in your journey, you've absorbed dozens of tactical tools: tax advantages, real estate maneuvers, insurance plays, legal structures, and charitable instruments. But the transformation only takes root when you shift from a tactician to a steward.

A tactician asks: How do I save more, make more, keep more?

A steward asks: What am I building? Who does this serve? How does it grow beyond me?

Stewardship means you begin managing your resources with vision, not just ambition. You start prioritizing durability over flash, purpose over prestige. You recognize that wealth, real wealth, is a tool, not a trophy.

And when wielded wisely, it can ripple through generations, communities, and even nations.

This is your opportunity. Not just to retire early. But to live more fully. To become the architect of a life that doesn't just work, but means something.

A New Legacy Begins with One Conversation

You've now built a foundational blueprint: strategic, structured, sustainable. But wealth isn't fully real until it's communicated.

The truth is, many families fall apart not for lack of money, but for lack of clarity, communication, and shared purpose. Economic freedom is fragile if it exists only in your head.

For me, all of this planning wasn't theoretical; it was urgent. It started with my heart stopping. Flatlining. The moment I realized that if I was gone, my family would have no plan, no guidance, no security. That health crisis was my wake-up call to do this work, to build structures, hold conversations, and pass on not just wealth but wisdom.

In the next chapter, we take everything you've learned and bring it home, literally. We'll talk about how to pass on values, not just valuables. How to create a Family Constitution, host a Financial Family Meeting, and write a Letter of Wishes that speaks louder than legal documents ever could.

Because ultimately, freedom isn't what you leave behind. It's what you pass forward, deliberately, lovingly, and boldly.

So as you turn the page, get ready to gather your loved ones around the table.

This time, not to talk about what's missing, but about what's possible.

That's why in the next chapter, we'll go deeper, beyond the numbers, into the psychology of wealth. You'll learn how belief systems, emotional intelligence, and mindset shape your financial outcomes more than any market or tax code ever will. Because before you can change your finances, you have to change the way you think. Let's explore that transformation next.

Chapter 13: The Psychology of wealth

When my heart stopped, my life didn't just flash before my eyes. It paused, demanding that I examine everything I believed.

I wasn't thinking about spreadsheets, accounts, or investment returns in that moment. I was thinking about my family: my wife Pallavi, my kids Anushka and Ashank. I realized that for all the effort I'd put into earning, I'd spent almost no time planning. And even less time asking why.

Why work so hard if you're not protecting what you build? Why sacrifice health for wealth, if you don't even believe you deserve to enjoy it?

Why hoard money if you're afraid to use it for the people and causes that matter most?

That heart crisis was more than a medical event. It was a psychological reckoning.

Because the truth is: Wealth begins in the mind long before it appears in your bank account.

You can have the best CPA, the most sophisticated trust, and a perfect investment strategy. But if your beliefs about money are broken, your results will be too.

This chapter is about that inner game. The psychology behind building, keeping, and *truly enjoying* wealth. Because before you change your finances, you have to change the way you think.

Mindset and Belief Systems

Most of us inherit our money mindset long before we realize it.

We hear things like:

- "Money doesn't grow on trees."
- "We can't afford that."
- "Rich people are greedy."
- "Play it safe."
- "Don't talk about money at the table."

We internalize these messages. They become invisible rules that shape every decision.

These rules aren't always true. But they're always powerful.

They can create a scarcity mindset: believing there's never enough, so hoarding instead of investing. Or a fear of success: guilt over earning more than your family or friends. Or fear of failure: paralyzed from starting a business or investing because of the chance of loss.

After my health crisis, I had to admit I had my own rules.

I told myself estate planning was for old people. That it was uncomfortable to talk about money with Pallavi. That I didn't have time to sit down with a CPA or tax planner.

But the truth was: I was afraid. Afraid of what it would mean to face my mortality. Afraid of admitting how unprepared I was.

Changing my financial future started with changing those beliefs.

Ask yourself:

- *What money beliefs did you inherit from your parents?*
- *Which of those serve you now?*
- *Which ones are holding you back?*

Because wealth isn't just numbers. It's the beliefs that shape how you earn, save, invest, and give.

Emotional Intelligence and Financial Decisions

Money is emotional.

No matter how rational we think we are, our financial decisions are often driven by fear, greed, pride, envy, shame, or guilt.

- Panic-selling in a downturn.
- Overleveraging because of FOMO.
- Avoiding talking about money with a spouse to avoid conflict.
- Underpricing your work because you don't believe in your value.

Emotional intelligence is your secret weapon.

It doesn't mean suppressing emotion. It means recognizing it. Naming it. Making sure it's not secretly running the show.

When my heart stopped, I felt fear, paralyzing fear, not just of dying, but of leaving my family with nothing but questions. That fear was useful, it forced me to act.

But too much fear paralyzes.

Too much shame prevents conversation.

Too much pride refuses help.

Emotional intelligence means:

- Noticing what you're feeling when you make a financial choice.
- Asking: *Is this fear? Is it wisdom?*
- Pausing before acting.
- Having open, sometimes vulnerable, conversations with people you trust.

It's why so much of this book isn't about secret hacks, but about communication.

Because wealth without emotional honesty is fragile.

Goal Setting and Visualization

Most people have vague goals about money.

"I want to be financially free."

"I want to retire early."

"I want to make more."

But vague goals create vague results. Specific goals create clear action.

Economic freedom isn't one number. It's the life that money enables.

- Time with your family.
- Helping your parents age with dignity.
- Funding your children's education.
- Traveling without debt.
- Giving generously to causes you love.

After my health scare, I didn't just say, "I need to get my affairs in order."

I visualized Pallavi and the kids sitting with an attorney after I died. Would they be confident? Or lost?

That image was painful, but it was clarifying.

It showed me why I needed a trust, life insurance, a will, a clear plan. It wasn't for me. It was for them.

Visualization isn't magic. It's clarity.

Ask yourself:

- *What does your ideal financially free life actually look like?*
- *How much does it cost?*
- *What needs to change to get there?*

Goals are your map. Visualization is your compass. Without them, even the best strategies go unused.

Overcoming Limiting Beliefs

Even with clear goals, many of us hit a ceiling.

- "People like me don't get rich."
- "I'm not good with money."
- "Taxes will always eat it all anyway."
- "I don't deserve more."

These are limiting beliefs.

They're often invisible. They might sound "reasonable." But they cap your potential.

After my heart event, I realized I had limiting beliefs too:

- That talking about money was uncomfortable.
- That I didn't know enough to plan.
- That I wasn't "qualified" to teach my children about wealth.

Overcoming limiting beliefs starts with noticing them.

Write them down. Challenge them:

- *Is this really true?*
- *Where did I learn it?*
- *What would I tell my child if they believed this?*

Replace them with empowering beliefs:

- "I can learn."
- "My family deserves clarity."
- "Wealth is stewardship, not greed."

Changing your beliefs isn't about lying to yourself. It's about giving yourself permission to grow.

Cultivating a Growth Mindset

Carol Dweck's research on mindset is clear:

A fixed mindset says:

- "I'm bad with money."
- "I can't understand taxes."
- "Investing is gambling."
- "That's only for the rich."

A growth mindset says:

- "I can learn about money."
- "I can ask for help."
- "I can make mistakes and get better."
- "I can build wealth in my own way."

Every strategy in this book demands a growth mindset.

Reading about taxes won't make you a CPA, but it makes you smart enough to hire one well.

Talking to an attorney once doesn't make you a lawyer, but it protects your family forever.

Learning about insurance doesn't make you an agent, but it makes you a better buyer.

After my heart scare, I had to choose growth over comfort.

I had to sit down with a tax planner and admit I didn't know enough.

I had to hold awkward conversations with Pallavi about life insurance.

I had to make time for estate attorneys when work was busy.

I had to teach my children about money when I was still learning myself.

It was uncomfortable. It was humbling. It was essential.

Growth isn't a destination. It's a choice you make again and again.

Your Wealth. Your Mindset. Your Legacy.

In the end, all wealth planning is personal development in disguise.

Because planning forces you to ask:

- What do I want?
- Who do I love?
- What am I protecting?
- What am I teaching?
- What legacy am I leaving?

Your mindset is what will decide:

- Whether you call the advisor.
- Whether you sit down for the family meeting.
- Whether you write the plan.
- Whether you teach your kids what you wish you'd known.

Wealth is a choice. So is poverty.

And that choice happens in your mind before it happens in your wallet.

If you remember nothing else from this book, remember this:

You don't need to be perfect. You need to be intentional.

Because the real wealth you're building isn't just for you. It's for the people who will one day ask:

How did you do it?

And you'll be ready to answer:

I didn't just plan. I believed.

I didn't just earn. I learned.

I didn't just save. I led.

I chose.

Chapter 14: The Authors Journey

When my heart stopped, everything changed.

People think that's just a saying. For me, it was literal. My heart rate dropped to zero. I flatlined. I had to be revived. More than once.

It wasn't a heart attack, but Bradycardia. A silent, creeping threat that forced itself into my life in the most violent way possible.

Today, I walk around with a pacemaker inside me, a small machine that beats for me, so I can keep living.

And every single beat it gives me feels borrowed. Precious.

It was in that hospital bed, surrounded by machines, fear, and the cold smell of antiseptic, that I had my true wake-up call.

Not about health, though that was urgent.

About *life*.

About *money*.

About *family*.

Because for all the working, earning, hustling, and providing I'd done...I had no plan. No will. No trust. No insurance that actually covered the worst-case scenario. No real roadmap.

If I had died in that bed, my family wouldn't just have lost me. They would have lost stability.

They would have faced courts. Probate. Taxes. Confusion. Stress on top of grief.

That moment is the reason this book exists.

I want you to feel the urgency I felt, without the terror I had to experience to get there.

Life After the Wake-Up Call

It's easy to imagine that once you have a life-changing moment, everything fixes itself.

It doesn't.

Life after that wake-up call wasn't perfect. It was raw. Uncomfortable. It meant finally talking about things I'd avoided.

With Pallavi. With my children. With myself.

I didn't become a financial expert overnight. But I became obsessed with learning.

Because when you almost die, you realize what you're really leaving behind. And I wasn't willing to leave my family with uncertainty.

My wake-up call taught me that wealth is not just about assets. It's about clarity. Communication. Intention.

It's about ensuring that if you're gone, those you love know what to do next.

Lessons Learned and Applied

Here's what I actually did. Not theory. Not platitudes. The real, unglamorous work that followed:

I built an estate plan. I met with attorneys. I sat through the explanations. I signed the documents. It wasn't fun. It wasn't sexy. But now there's a clear plan for what happens if I'm not here.

I set up a Trust and Will. So, my family wouldn't face the nightmare of probate. So, they'd know exactly what assets go where. So, there would be no fighting, no guessing, no courts deciding for us.

I put insurance in place. Not just one policy, but layers of it, Term Life for big coverage at low cost. Whole Life for permanent coverage and cash value. Indexed Universal Life (IUL) for flexibility and growth.

I designed an IRA to Roth Conversion Plan. To reduce taxes in retirement, so future withdrawals would be tax-free, even if tax rates rise.

I started investing deliberately to reduce taxable income. Using strategies you've read about in this book, real estate, depreciation, bonus depreciation, Section 179. I stopped being passive about taxes.

I bought a business. Not just for income, but to teach my children what ownership really means. How to manage. How to lead. How to think long-term.

I sat my family down. We had the talk. The Family Meeting. I walked them through what I had done. Where the documents were. Who to call? What to expect.

I wrote this book. Because I knew there were thousands of people like me, working hard, earning well, but unprepared. I couldn't live with knowing I had survived but stayed silent.

I started a nonprofit. So, proceeds from this book and other efforts could help others. So my family could see giving back as part of our legacy.

I invested in legacy wealth. Not just real estate, but digital assets like cryptocurrency. Diversifying. Thinking about the future, not just the present.

I built a team. A CPA, a Tax Planner, an Estate Attorney. I stopped trying to do everything alone and found professionals who could help me do it right.

Ongoing Financial Planning and Adoption

One of the biggest lessons I learned?

This work doesn't end.

Financial planning is not a one-time event.

It's a habit.

It's quarterly meetings with Pallavi to review accounts, insurance, documents, and contacts.

It's annual sit-downs with the CPA to review our taxes before the year ends, not after.

It's revisiting our goals as the kids grow, as markets change, as our needs evolve.

It's staying curious. Staying humble. Staying open to learning.

The wake-up call didn't just force me to plan once. It forced me to commit to always planning.

Because life doesn't stand still. Neither should your strategy.

Giving Back and Sharing Knowledge

When I was recovering, I had a lot of dark nights.

I thought: Why me? Why did this happen?

Over time, the question changed:

Why not me?

If it hadn't been me, I wouldn't have woken up. I wouldn't have learned. I wouldn't have built this plan.

Maybe my story can be the warning sign someone else listens to before they have to live through the same fear.

That's why I wrote this book.

Not because I'm a CPA. Not because I'm a financial advisor. But because I'm a husband. A father. A survivor.

Someone who almost left it all behind in chaos, and who refused to let that stand.

My nonprofit is designed to keep this mission going. Proceeds from this book, speaking engagements, and partnerships will go into helping others plan. Into scholarships. Medical outreach. Education.

Because knowledge is only power if it's shared.

A Look Ahead: Future Goals and Aspirations

So what now?

My journey isn't over.

My goals today aren't just about growing net worth. They're about deepening meaning.

- **Teaching my kids.** Not just giving them assets, but skills. Conversations. Values.
- **Supporting my wife.** Ensuring Pallavi always feels confident and included in our plan.
- **Expanding our giving.** Funding the nonprofit so it outlives me.
- **Investing in the future.** New markets. Crypto. Sustainable ventures.

- **Staying healthy.** Honoring this second chance by caring for my body and mind.
- **Spreading the word.** Speaking. Teaching. Inspiring others to avoid my mistakes.

Because true wealth isn't about having more. It's about meaning more.

Final Words to You

If you've read this far, thank you.

Thank you for giving me the chance to share not just what I learned, but why I learned it.

My hope isn't that you copy everything I did, line for line. My hope is that you think.

That you act.

That you don't leave your family guessing.

That you don't wait for a hospital bed to force you to get serious.

That you recognize your power to change your story.

Because you do have power.

You can build a plan.

You can teach your children.

You can protect your spouse.

You can support your community.

You can leave a legacy that outlives you.

This is my journey.

It's messy. Honest. Imperfect.

But it's mine.

Now it's your turn.

Pick up the pen.

Write yours.

Chapter 15: Conclusion: Building your secure financial future

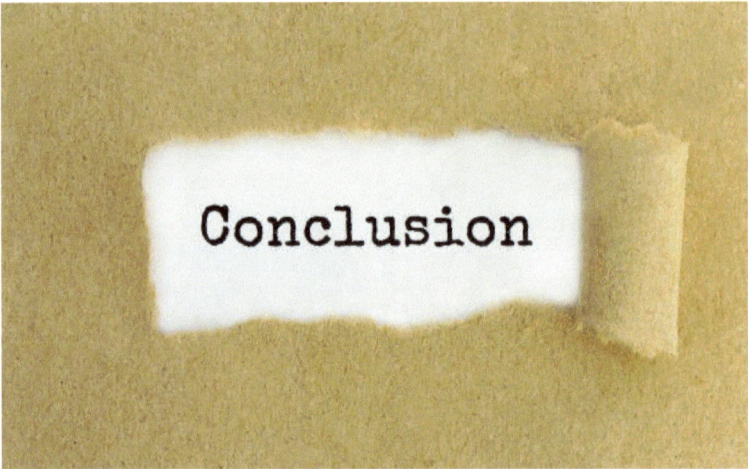

We've covered a lot of ground together.

If you're still reading, I want to say one thing above all else: thank you for caring enough about yourself, your family, and your future to make it this far.

This isn't an easy topic. Most people would rather ignore it, push it off, or pretend everything will somehow "work out."

But you didn't.

You showed up.

You read.

You thought.

And hopefully, you're ready to act.

Because that's what this is really about.

Not knowing. But doing.

Recap of Key Strategies

Throughout this book, you've learned more than just theory. You've received a blueprint, a real plan to build a secure, tax-smart, resilient financial future.

Let's remember some of the key strategies you now hold in your toolkit:

- **Tax Planning:** Leveraging deductions, credits, Section 179, bonus depreciation, cost segregation, and timing strategies like Section 461. Using structures like S-Corps, LLCs, and C-Corps for maximum efficiency.
- **Wealth Building Vehicles:** Real estate investing, heavy equipment, oil and gas, short-term rentals, syndications, REITs, and 1031 exchanges.

- **Insurance as a Wealth Tool:** Using Whole Life and Indexed UL to become your own bank, build intergenerational wealth, and provide certainty.
- **Estate Planning:** Trusts, wills, letters of wishes, family constitutions, and layered asset protection to preserve your legacy.
- **Charitable Strategies:** Donor-Advised Funds, CRTs, Qualified Charitable Distributions, direct appreciated asset donations, and building your own 501(c)(3) to give back while reducing taxes.
- **Retirement Optimization:** IRA to Roth conversions, ROBS and SDIRA strategies, ERISA plans, and mega-backdoor Roth contributions.
- **Mindset and Communication:** Hosting family meetings, teaching your kids about money, creating transparency with your spouse, and aligning your values with your financial plan.

These aren't just tactics. They're building blocks for freedom.

The Importance of Ongoing Planning

If there's one thing I learned from my health scare, it's this:

Planning isn't one-and-done.

Your life will change. Your income will change. Your goals will evolve. The tax code will shift.

That means your plan has to evolve too.

It's not enough to set up a trust once and forget about it. Or buy insurance and never review your coverage. Or make an investment without monitoring it.

Financial security is a habit, not an event.

That's why my family and I hold quarterly check-ins.
It's why I talk to my CPA before the year ends.
It's why we update documents when our lives change.
It's why we keep talking, so no one is left in the dark.

Ongoing planning isn't extra work. It's peace of mind.

Embracing the Journey

If I'm honest, a part of me wishes I could tell you this work is easy.

But it's not.

It will challenge you. It will ask you to have hard conversations. It will push you to face your fears about mortality, conflict, and even your own limitations.

But there's beauty in that.

Because wealth planning isn't just about money. It's about meaning.

It's about asking yourself:

- What do I want to leave behind?
- Who do I want to protect?
- What example do I want to set?
- How do I want to be remembered?

If you can embrace those questions, you can embrace the entire journey.

Because this isn't about getting rich for its own sake.

It's about building a life that matters.

Taking Action and Next Steps

Reading this book is only step one.

Step two is action.

Here's what I hope you'll do:

- Review what you have in place. Be honest about the gaps.
- Schedule the meeting with your attorney to draft or update your will and trust.
- Talk to a CPA who understands proactive, strategic tax planning.
- Sit with your spouse or partner and share everything, accounts, passwords, advisors.
- Host the family meeting you've been avoiding.
- Teach your children what you wish you'd known.
- Build a team around you. Don't go it alone.
- Set goals. Review them. Adjust them as life changes.

You don't have to do it all tomorrow.

But you do have to start.

Because no one else will do it for you.

Final Reflection: Living a Purposeful Life

My journey didn't start with a love for tax law.

It started with my heart stopping.

It started with the terrifying realization that I might leave my family unprepared.

It started with asking:

What happens to them if I'm not here?

And the answer was unacceptable.

That moment changed me. It forced me to do the work. To have the conversations. To build the plan.

And to share it with you.

Because in the end, wealth is not about how much you have.

It's about how well you live.

It's not about the size of your portfolio. It's about the strength of your plan.

It's not about avoiding taxes just to keep more. It's about using every dollar to build something meaningful.

It's not about making your family rich. It's about making them ready.

It's not about leaving behind money. It's about leaving behind clarity. Values. Security. Love.

Wealth is a choice. So is legacy.

My hope is that you choose both.

Thank you for letting me share my story.

Now it's time to write your own.

Live well. Plan well. And leave something that lasts.

www.ingramcontent.com/pod-product-compliance
Lightning Source LLC
Chambersburg PA
CBHW041004210326
41597CB00001B/10